# QUIET TIME
# MOMENTS
## *for*
# WOMEN

# QUIET TIME
# MOMENTS
## *for*
# WOMEN

## CATHERINE
## MARTIN

HARVEST HOUSE PUBLISHERS

EUGENE, OREGON

*Cover by Koechel Peterson & Associates, Inc., Minneapolis, Minnesota*

Published in association with the literary agency of WordServe Literary Group, Ltd., 10152 S. Knoll Circle, Highlands Ranch, CO 80130

**QUIET TIME MOMENTS FOR WOMEN**
Copyright © 2010 by Catherin Martin
Published by Harvest House Publishers
Eugene, Oregon 97402
www.harvesthousepublishers.com

ISBN 978-0-7369-2922-6

**Printed in China**

10 11 12 13 14 15 16 17 18 / RDS-SK / 10 9 8 7 6 5 4 3 2 1

To Leann McGee
Thank you for teaching me about quiet time
early on in my relationship with God.
You have shown me how to faithfully follow Christ.
Your name is written next to Hebrews 13:7 in my Bible,
and I will always thank the Lord for the gift of you in my life.

# Contents

# Introduction

I sat with 30 other Christian students from Arizona State University as a man talked with us about commitment to Christ. Suddenly he stopped and looked into our young faces. Then he said, "In ten years, only a few of you will be walking closely with the Lord." We were shocked. We looked at each other and thought, *No way! We love the Lord!* But his prediction was accurate.

I've noticed that there are two kinds of Christians—those who walk closely with Christ and those who don't. I've also discovered that our time alone with God determines the intimacy of our relationship with Him.

Many years ago, Leann McGee, a staff member with Campus Crusade for Christ, gave me one of the best gifts I've ever received: quiet time. Spending quiet time with God is one of my favorite joys each day. My daily time alone with God has been one of the primary sources of the strength I need to keep from giving up in the most difficult times in my life. When I've drawn near to God, opened the pages of His Word, and heard Him speak, I've enjoyed the Holy Spirit's transforming power in my heart. When I miss my daily quiet time, I know I have missed the truth God had prepared for me that day. More than that, I've missed intimate communion with the Lord. And yet God is gracious and always longs for my fellowship. He says, "Be still, and know that I am God" (Psalm 46:10 niv).

Spiritual breakthroughs occur daily when we get quiet and listen to God speak in His Word. God has something to say to us if we are willing to stop long enough to sit with Him awhile and listen. If we truly realize God's desire for intimacy with us, we'll set aside many good things for the very best times imaginable with the Creator of the universe.

As founder of Quiet Time Ministries, I talk a lot about quiet time, meditating in God's Word, writing in a journal, using a quiet time notebook, and praying with the Lord. My sharing flows from a passion for quiet time with my Lord. The books I've written and messages I've given have come from simple yet profound and life-changing devotional delights in my day—quiet times.

For many years now, I've kept a written record of the spiritual nuggets of truth I've discovered in the Word. Yearly, I like to choose a word and a verse to focus on as I walk with the Lord. I've chosen words like *trust, hope, faith,* and *love.* Throughout the year, God plants many spiritual seeds that yield a harvest of spiritual truth on each topic.

*Quiet Time Moments for Women* is a collection of devotions based on some of the most important words and topics I've discovered in the Bible during my own quiet times. Each reading contains a spiritual nugget— a simple but profound truth—gleaned from some of my favorite verses in the Bible. Every devotion includes elements from the PRAYER quiet time plan I wrote about in *Six Secrets to a Powerful Quiet Time*:

> Prepare Your Heart
>
> Read and Study God's Word
>
> Adore God in Prayer
>
> Yield Yourself to God
>
> Enjoy His Presence
>
> Rest in His Love

These meditations will prepare your heart to meet with the Lord and encourage you in difficult days. Take time with each verse, open your Bible, underline your favorite words and phrases, meditate on the devotion, and think about its application in your own life throughout the day. By the time you finish your journey with the Lord through this devotional, you will have gathered up a wealth of treasure.

God bless you as you draw near to your Lord. May you enjoy a more intimate relationship with your awesome, majestic, glorious Lord and God!

In His love,
*Catherine Martin*

# QUIET

# Come Away

Come away with me by yourselves to
a quiet place and rest a little while.

**MARK 6:31 WILLIAMS**

---

The disciples had just completed their first missionary trip. They told Jesus everything they had accomplished. How would He respond? Would He send them out again after their good report? Jesus, by example and words, teaches every disciple of His what to do when life gets busy. He said, "Come away with Me."

You've undoubtedly experienced times when you had so much on your plate that you didn't even know where to begin. Your task list is sometimes longer than the hours in a day. Do you know what the opposite of *busy* is? *Quiet.* A quiet place was the special location Jesus had in mind for His followers on that event-filled day.

Are you busy right now in your own life? Can you hear Jesus inviting you, even imploring you, "Come away with Me" to a quiet place and rest a little while? Will you say yes to His invitation today?

*Lord, I want to come away with*
*You to a quiet place today. Amen.*

# Come to Me

Come to Me, all who are weary and
heavy-laden, and I will give you rest.

**MATTHEW 11:28**

-----------------------------

How's your heart these days? No one knows your heart better than Jesus does. He often sees extreme exhaustion and heavy burdens in hearts. He doesn't condemn. Instead, His soothing words prescribe the appropriate treatment. When He speaks, He comforts and heals aching, heavy hearts. He invites us, "Come to Me, all who are weary and heavy-laden…" There's the prescription. And then the soothing balm, "I will give you rest." Imagine Jesus speaking these very words to you today. Don't you long for a real rest in your weary heart and soul?

How will you respond to Jesus? His invitation is so winsome, so appealing, that perhaps you are ready to drop everything immediately and escape with Him to a place of solitude for blessed communion with your Lord. Why not schedule some uninterrupted time alone with Him now? You can enjoy a renewed heart and a refreshed spirit.

*Lord, I look forward to a refreshing
time alone with You. Amen.*

# Strength in the Quiet

In repentance and rest you will be saved,
In quietness and trust is your strength.

**ISAIAH 30:15**

-----------------------------

Sometimes we think if we handle a problem quickly, it will disappear. Have you noticed that quick reactions often complicate rather than resolve situations? In the prophet Isaiah's time, God's people were in trouble because they trusted themselves and others rather than trusting the Lord. Many people live the same way today, thinking they can run their own lives. Then, when the troubles of life stack up, answers are nowhere to be found.

What will help when you are overwhelmed in life? Return to God and discover real rest. Step away from the trouble and run into the quiet place with your Lord. There, in the quiet, you will find a new reliance on your Lord. Then you will experience His wisdom and strength, equal to any task or difficulty.

*Lord, today I'm stopping everything for time alone with You. Fill me with Your strength and power. Amen.*

# What Would God Say?

Be still, and know that I am God.

**PSALM 46:10 NKJV**

---

Have you ever wished you could hear from God in the midst of a trial? You can know His words because He has written a love letter to you. When you read the Bible, you can gain a glimpse into His heart. Some of the best words you will ever hear Him say are these: "Be still, and know that I am God." These words apply in every situation. He is inviting you to stop everything, relax, and be still. If you continue to run at breakneck speed, rushing through your daily responsibilities, you will miss the main truths in your life: who God is, what He does, and what He says. Slowing down and stopping long enough to draw near to God will help you see the truth that God is infinite, eternal, and all-powerful. He is enough for whatever you face in your life. Think on His simple yet profound words today: "I am God." He is the One you need every day.

*Lord, I need You today, and I rely on You. Amen.*

# Your Quiet Time

But Jesus Himself would often slip
away to the wilderness and pray.

**LUKE 5:16**

-------------------------------------

L arge crowds gathered to hear Jesus and be healed of
their diseases. His own brothers encouraged Him
to seize the moment and take advantage of His popu-
larity. But Jesus walked a different path in life. He often slipped away to the wilderness and prayed. Jesus was
in the habit of spending quiet time with His heavenly
Father. If quiet time was important for Jesus, it certainly
must be for you and me. A consistent habit of quiet time
is not easy to cultivate, for there are many good distractions waiting to fill up your day. But even Jesus needed
to "slip away" to enjoy necessary quiet in the wilderness.
Ask God to help you spend time with Him every day.
Schedule a daily time with your Lord. Then look for
those moments when you can slip away to enjoy fellowship with Jesus. Blessed communion with Jesus will
feed your soul and refresh your spirit.

*Lord, thank You for encouragement to slip away*
*to a quiet place and talk with You. Amen.*

# When Can You Be with Jesus?

*Now in the morning, having risen a long while*
*before daylight, He went out and departed*
*to a solitary place; and there He prayed.*

**MARK 1:35 NKJV**

Jesus was intentional in His quiet time, choosing the early morning to get alone and talk with God. When is your best time for uninterrupted time with the Lord? You may be thinking, *I can't. My responsibilities are too overwhelming.*

Consider Susannah Wesley, mother of 19 children. She stood in the middle of her kitchen, threw her apron over her head, and talked with her Lord there in the quiet of a cloth sanctuary. When the children saw their mother with the apron over her head, they knew they must wait, for she was talking with God. Susannah Wesley's example speaks to every busy woman: "It's possible. You can find a way. Even in this season of your life." So grab an apron if you must and find some quiet time with God where you will renew your spirit, refresh your heart, and revive your soul.

*Lord, thank You for Your example in my*
*life today. I look forward to knowing You*
*better and loving You more. Amen.*

# The Solitary Place

In the early morning, while it was still dark,
Jesus got up, left the house, and went away
to a secluded place, and was praying there.

**MARK 1:35**

-------------------------------

When Jesus spent time with His Father, He chose a secluded, solitary place for prayer. A quiet place helps you slow down to hear God speak. Noise drowns out deep thoughts. In the solitude and silence of a quiet place, you can think about the meaning of God's Word and its application in your life.

Where will you find undisturbed time away from distractions? Where can you commune with the Lord? Maybe your back porch would offer a quiet place for you. Sometimes even the corner table of a coffee shop provides just the privacy needed for alone time with God. Or maybe you can find a picnic table in a park. Wherever you find your quiet place, you will discover a river of blessings as God renews your heart through communion with Him.

*Lord, in the solitude of our quiet time together,*
*renew my mind and heart. Amen.*

# Times of Refreshing

Repent and return, so that your sins may be
wiped away, in order that times of refreshing
may come from the presence of the Lord.

**ACTS 3:19**

---

Do you need a time of rest and refreshing? Imagine finding a pool of water on a hot day. When you run to the Lord, you will find His presence so powerful that you are invigorated and energized. Perhaps a time of renewal seems impossible. With God all things are possible—even refreshment in your own life.

One of the ways God refreshes you is with His Word (Psalm 119:50). When you open the pages of the Bible, you are handling the living, active Word of God (Hebrews 4:12). The Bible will continually encourage you to come near to Jesus and live in His presence. When you are with Jesus, your circumstances seem different, and you see possibilities and opportunities that you may not have seen before. Take some time now and draw near, asking Jesus to refresh your heart.

*Lord, thank You for Your Word, which is powerful*
*enough to refresh me with Your presence. Amen.*

# When Everything Changes

God is our refuge and strength,
A very present help in trouble.

**PSALM 46:1**

-----------------------------

What can quiet your heart when everything around you changes? Run to God, your refuge and strength. He will help you in your trouble.

Imagine walking along when suddenly dark clouds fill the sky and rain begins to fall. Soon the storm is so great that you must find shelter before you become completely drenched. Many changes in your world come upon you like an unexpected rainstorm. In the storms of life, God is your shelter, a safe place to hide when the winds and rain threaten to wash you away. He is always with you to help whenever you need Him. God's knowledge is infinite, and His plan is perfect. So if you encounter any surprising changes in your life today, remember to take shelter in your perfect refuge and find a quiet place to rest.

*Lord, thank You for being my refuge and strength, a very present help in times of trouble. I take comfort in Your protection and security today. Amen.*

# Choosing the Best

Only one thing is necessary, for Mary
has chosen the good part, which shall
not be taken away from her.

**LUKE 10:42**

---

Martha and Mary were sisters and Jesus' friends. When Jesus visited their house, Martha was distracted with preparations, but Mary was focused. Martha was worried and bothered about many things, but Mary was sitting at the Lord's feet, listening to His word. Jesus applauded Mary and said she had chosen the one necessary thing in life.

Today, are you more like Martha or Mary? Every day you choose. Resolve to be a Mary. Open the Bible, sit at Jesus' feet, and hear Him speak to you. Just think about the day when you step from time into eternity and see Jesus. What joy will fill your heart when you realize firsthand your better choice in life! In eternity, the many good things fade away, and the one best choice—Jesus—shines so brightly that He lights up all of heaven.

*Lord, help me choose to take time each day to open
Your Word, sit at Your feet, and listen to You. Amen.*

# Remain in Jesus

Abide in Me, and I in you.

**JOHN 15:4**

---

When Jesus asks you to come to Him, He invites you to stay forever. Your relationship with Him is not a "come and go" kind of connection, but a vital, abiding communion with eternal results. When you remain in Him, you thrive and bear fruit. Quiet time every day helps you abide in Christ, experience the amazing impact of His abiding words in you, and see Him personally answer your prayers (John 15:7).

Jesus likens Himself to the true vine. You are like a branch drawing necessary nutrients from Him. When the branch is fully connected to the vine, the wood is strong and able to withstand the elements, grow, and bear more fruit. When you remain in vital contact with Jesus, you can triumph in fierce storms and fiery trials. If you feel threatened by a storm today, run to Jesus and experience His strength, joy, and peace.

*Lord, I'm excited to abide in You, and I look forward to our intimate fellowship throughout this day. Amen.*

# Real Peace

Peace I leave with you; My peace I give to you;
not as the world gives do I give to you. Do not
let your heart be troubled, nor let it be fearful.

**JOHN 14:27**

---

Jesus promises you peace and gives you a tranquil and quiet calmness of mind even in the midst of adversity. The story is told of a famous artist who was asked to paint the perfect representation of peace. He confidently displayed his painting, declaring with conviction, "Now *this* is peace." The canvas was filled with dark storm clouds, rain pouring down, and a bent tree, blown over by the wind. A closer look revealed a nest in a knothole in the tree and a mother bird sitting calmly with her chicks, undisturbed by the storm. Jesus' peace works the same way in your life. Even in the storm, you can enjoy undisturbed tranquility when you know His peace.

*Lord, thank You for Your promise of peace.*
*Help me trust You to keep me steady and*
*give me peace in turbulent times. Amen.*

# In the Wilderness

I will lead her into the desert and
speak tenderly to her there.

**HOSEA 2:14 NIV**

---

Are you in the desert right now? Maybe you are in the wilderness and desperately desire life in the garden. Be encouraged—the wilderness can become a garden. God promises springs in the valleys and water in the wilderness (Isaiah 41:18). When God led His people into the desert, He promised He would speak to their hearts. The desert can become a sanctuary when you meet with the Lord there. Some of God's words are understood only in the desert places. God's fellowship is so much sweeter when nothing competes with His presence. A light always shines more brightly in the darkness. If you are in a wilderness, listen closely to God's Word. Spiritual breakthroughs often come in the wilderness, where God speaks tenderly, holding you close to His heart.

*Lord, thank You that You are close to the
brokenhearted and speak to me even when I am in
the desert. I am listening for You even now. Amen.*

# The Valley of Tears

When they walk through the Valley of Weeping,
it will become a place of refreshing springs.

**PSALM 84:6 NLT**

No one asks God for the valley experience or the dark night of the soul. But your pilgrimage may include travel through the valley of weeping, where tears become your close friends day and night. A promise remains for any who walk through the valley of weeping. In God's time, your valley transforms into refreshing springs. Tears turn into triumph, and refreshment cleanses your soul. Ultimately, you will enjoy blessings known only deep in the valley. You did not want to go there, but when you receive God's special valley blessings, you change your mind. God's majesty sparkles in deepest wells, for His glory does not depend on favorable circumstances. He has been known to surprise valiant warriors who weep, for He promises His presence to the brokenhearted (Psalm 34:18). Today, remember all God's blessings in the valley of tears.

*Lord, thank You for the promise of refreshing
springs in the valley of weeping. Amen.*

# Have You Found Your Real Home?

God is bedrock under my feet,
the castle in which I live.

**PSALM 18:2 MSG**

------------------------------

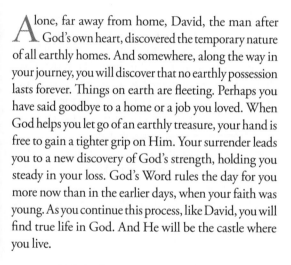

Alone, far away from home, David, the man after God's own heart, discovered the temporary nature of all earthly homes. And somewhere, along the way in your journey, you will discover that no earthly possession lasts forever. Things on earth are fleeting. Perhaps you have said goodbye to a home or a job you loved. When God helps you let go of an earthly treasure, your hand is free to gain a tighter grip on Him. Your surrender leads you to a new discovery of God's strength, holding you steady in your loss. God's Word rules the day for you more now than in the earlier days, when your faith was young. As you continue this process, like David, you will find true life in God. And He will be the castle where you live.

*Lord, thank You for being my real home, an eternal place, untouched and unmoved in the midst of a temporary, changing world. Amen.*

# Treasure in the Darkness

I will give you treasures hidden
in the darkness—secret riches.
I will do this so you may know that I am the LORD,
the God of Israel, the one who calls you by name.

**ISAIAH 45:3 NLT**

---

Hidden in the darkness of a trial are promised treasures, secret riches from the Lord. Some of God's best blessings are reserved for those who suffer. Only those who walk in darkness can enjoy the treasures hidden in the night. God calls those in the darkness by name. There's your first treasure: God knows your name. Even if you feel alone, you are never alone, for God is with you, calling out to you. In the quiet places of darkness, you can more easily hear the Lord whisper your name.

Hidden treasures can be like bright spots in dark places. So look for the treasure and listen for the One who calls you by name.

*Lord, I stand amazed at Your ways. Thank You for the treasures hidden in darkness. I am listening for You today. Amen.*

# A Song in the Night

Where is God my Maker,
Who gives songs in the night?

**JOB 35:10**

------------------------------

David had been running from King Saul for many months. He realized Saul intended to kill him. So he took the path he had avoided, knowing it was his only hope for survival. He traveled into enemy territory, hoping for safety behind enemy lines. And now, David, the man after God's own heart, sank into the miry pit of despair. He cried out, "O LORD, how long will you forget me? Forever?" (Psalm 13:1 NLT).

Have you ever felt like David? The whole world is seemingly against you. No one seems to respect or care for you. Be encouraged—God gives songs even in the night. Job found his song in the discovery of his Maker. David found a song from the Lord when he experienced God's goodness. God's unfailing love arranged an amazing rescue. And oh, how David sang—and you will too.

*Lord, thank You in advance for Your rescue. Your goodness and unfailing love are unparalleled. Give me a new song in my dark night. Amen.*

# Sitting at the Lord's Table

Behold, I stand at the door and knock;
if anyone hears My voice and opens the door,
I will come in to him and will dine
with him, and he with Me.

**REVELATION 3:20**

------------

Can you imagine the delightful experience of walking into your favorite restaurant, finding the best table, and discovering Jesus waiting for you?

In His company, all earthly fears seem to fade into the background, and your love for Him grows. To know Jesus is to love Him. Jesus never stops initiating in your relationship with Him. He notices when you are distant and knocks at the door of your life. Will you hear Him asking for entrance? And then will you open the door and say, *Come in, Lord*? If so, then prepare for time alone with Jesus at His table. Today, open the door and welcome Jesus into your life. A feast awaits.

*Lord, thank You for continually knocking and initiating in our relationship. Welcome into my life today. I look forward to our feast at Your table. Amen.*

# Soul Thirst

As the deer pants for the water brooks,
So my soul pants for You, O God.
My soul thirsts for God, for the living God.

**PSALM 42:1-2**

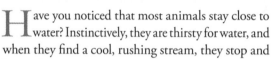

Have you noticed that most animals stay close to water? Instinctively, they are thirsty for water, and when they find a cool, rushing stream, they stop and linger there.

How thirsty are you for God these days? How can you measure your spiritual thirst? When you are spiritually thirsty, you think about God through the day. Certain verses from the Bible may come to your mind, turning your thoughts to the Lord. Your time with God may be sporadic, yet your heart's desire is intimacy with Him. Take a lesson from the deer satisfying their thirst at the water brooks. Come to the water of God and His Word and drink deeply from the Lord's cup. Once you have tasted of the Lord, you will never settle for less than His living water in your life.

*Lord, thank You for the living water,*
*quenching my deepest thirst. Amen.*

# The Courts of the Lord

A day in Your courts is better
than a thousand outside.

**PSALM 84:10**

-----------------------------------

Do you feel as though you have faced some tough choices lately? Life is filled with choices. And sometimes we need to say no to a good opportunity in order to say yes to the best one. The Lord will help you make good decisions. Here's a good question to ask: Does this line up with God's ways and encourage me to draw near to Him?

One psalmist chose a day in the Lord's courts instead of a thousand outside. On the surface, who wouldn't choose a day in the Lord's courts? What a seemingly easy choice. But somehow, without realizing it, a struggle often ensues in our lives between our daily responsibilities and our time with the Lord in His courts. The choice is between something that's *good* and something that's *better*. Always remember, time with the Lord in His courts is better than a thousand outside.

*Lord, today I choose Your courts and*
*delight in Your presence. Amen.*

# Loving God's Presence

How lovely are Your dwelling places,
O LORD of hosts!

**PSALM 84:1**

When you come to the quiet place with your Lord, you will see His beauty. Oh, how lovely He is. His glory will bring you to your knees in adoration and worship. Open the pages of your Bible, and every chapter will reveal truths about who God is, what God does, and what He says. You can never open the Bible without finding a new window into God's character. He is stunning and awesome. The eternal and uncreated Lord, fierce in His majesty and holy in His magnificence, produces awe and reverence in hearts. The more you spend time with God, the more humble you will become. And you will find a deep love for Him growing until one day you realize He has commanded your allegiance. You love Him passionately with all your heart, soul, mind, and strength. The psalmist knew this growing love, and you can too.

*Lord, I love being close to You and desire to know*
*You and love You with all my heart. Amen.*

# No More Night

There will no longer be any night.

**REVELATION 22:5**

---

Someday there will be no more night, no more storms, pain, or suffering. There will be no death, mourning, or tears. You will enjoy God in a whole new way in heaven, for you will see His face. This vision of eternity was given to John, the beloved apostle, to pass along to the suffering, persecuted church. A vision of eternity gives hope and endurance to suffering believers. The promise of no more night helps you see the rest of your story. Your promised future in heaven gives you the truth you need to press through your present trials. This life is not all there is, nor is it the best there is. You have a future and a hope with your Lord in paradise, where the Son always shines. He is the light of heaven and the light in your heart even now.

*Lord, thank You for being the light of the world and the bright, shining light in my life. Amen.*

# Your Life Is a Journey

Your life is a journey you must travel
with a deep consciousness of God.

**1 PETER 1:17 MSG**

---------------------------------

In John Bunyan's classic allegory *The Pilgrim's Progress*, the main character, Christian, is weighed down with a heavy burden. He meets Evangelist, who points him to a gate, promising hope and relief somewhere on the other side. Christian leaves everything to be freed of his burden. When he experiences deliverance, the straps that bind his burden to him break, and he is freed from the weight of sin. Then begins his real journey through difficult territories, where he encounters more challenges. But finally, Christian reaches his destination, the Celestial City.

Bunyan's beloved allegory reminds us that life is truly a journey. Peter encourages fellow journeyers to travel with a deep consciousness of God. You are never alone on your journey. God is always with you. He never abandons His people. Take comfort in His words to Moses: "My presence will go with you. I'll see the journey to the end" (Exodus 33:14 MSG).

*Lord, I'm excited to engage in this*
*journey with You. Amen.*

# Set Your Heart on Pilgrimage

Blessed are those whose strength is in you,
who have set their hearts on pilgrimage.

**PSALM 84:5 NIV**

---

God is issuing a call to His people to engage in a journey with Him—a pilgrimage of the heart. God's call to pilgrimage is a summons to find your home in Him and live in the world as one who journeys in a foreign land until you reach your grand destination, heaven. God's travelers set their hearts on pilgrimage. We might call this the *heart-set* of a Christian—a deep determination and resolve that flows as a passion from the heart. When you respond to God's pilgrim call, you resolve to find the source of life, which is Christ alone. So get ready for the journey. This great adventure of knowing God includes plenty of hills and valleys, but the view is breathtaking.

*Lord, I answer Your call today. I'm ready
to engage in Your adventure and can't
wait to traverse life with You. Amen.*

# Travelers in a Foreign Land

By faith he lived as an alien in the land
of promise, as in a foreign land.

**HEBREWS 11:9**

Now you are God's pilgrim. You join a great company of believers who have traveled with God throughout the ages. They set aside the things of the world to follow Christ.

Sometimes, life will seem strange and alien to you. Why? You are beginning to see how the world is unlike your real home with the Lord. When you walk with God, you breathe in the atmosphere of heaven. Therefore, you never really unpack your bags or put down roots here in the world. You realize you are traveling in a foreign land. Abraham knew the pilgrim journey and dwelt in a tent on his way to heaven. Always remember you are on a journey with God, and you will lose the compulsion to become like those in the world.

*Lord, I feel as though I am not at home here
in the world. Thank You that someday I will
breathe a sigh of relief when I am face-to-face
with You. I will say, "I'm finally home." Amen.*

# Traveling Companion

We will come and make our
home with each of them.

**JOHN 14:23 NLT**

---

W hen you travel as a pilgrim on a pilgrimage of the heart, you never journey alone. The triune God is traveling with you. You have the best traveling companion imaginable. The Creator of the universe, who can create something out of nothing, sets His artistry at work in you. Jesus, who loves you so much He gave His life for you, walks and talks with you. The Holy Spirit, called the Helper, indwells you and empowers you for every task.

How can you go wrong when the triune God is with you? You will discover, like Jeremiah, that God's faithfulness is great (Lamentations 3:22-23). His lovingkindness is everlasting, His compassions never fail, and His mercies are new every morning. Therefore, launch out in life with excitement and confidence, knowing God goes with you. He is faithful to lead you, guide you, and provide for you each moment of your journey.

*Lord, thank You for being my traveling
companion on this journey of life. Amen.*

# Traveling with God

And how blessed all those in whom you live,
whose lives become roads you travel.

**PSALM 84:5 MSG**

---

The journey of life is never boring when you travel with God. He adds the adventure of discovery, and He loves to surprise you. Always remember He is with you. He will offer a panorama of color and beauty to even the most tedious of tasks and drudgery in your days. Walk and talk with Him throughout your day, looking for Him in each moment.

How do you walk and talk with your Lord? Share with Him as you would with your best and dearest friend. Pour out your dreams, disappointments, delights, and yes, even your deepest despairs and greatest burdens. The Lord's loving-kindnesses never cease, and they are new every morning (Lamentations 3:22-23). When you give your burden to the Lord, you have less baggage, and then your travel is so much easier.

*Lord, thank You today for lifting my burden,*
*lightening my load, and leading me on this*
*great adventure of knowing You. Amen.*

# Packing Your Bags

Let us strip off every weight that slows us down.

**HEBREWS 12:1 NLT**

---

A young girl packed her bags for a missionary trip. She had never traveled before, so she packed items that would remind her of home. She included favorite books, pictures, and other memorabilia. Soon her small bag was filled, and she had not yet packed the necessary clothing. So she unpacked the small bag and opened up a larger suitcase. After stuffing every area of the new bag, she was able to close it only with the help of a friend. What do you think she discovered once her journey began? Her suitcase was so heavy she could barely move it, making her trip less than enjoyable. She had packed too much.

The writer of Hebrews encourages you to lay aside those weights that slow you down in your race. Ask the Lord today to show you every encumbrance and give you wisdom as you pack your bags.

> *Lord, show me the weights that are slowing me down in our journey together. Amen.*

# Faith Is Necessary

By faith these people overthrew
kingdoms, ruled with justice, and received
what God had promised for them.

**HEBREWS 11:33 NLT**

---

I n Hebrews 11, faith's hall of fame, we learn that faith
is one of the essential items to pack in our suitcases.
Paul said, "We walk by faith, not by sight" (2 Corinthians 5:7). Your journey is by faith, so you will need to
take faith with you. Faith will help you see God. Faith
enables you to grasp God's promises when you open the
Bible. And you will need God's promises, for they tether
your soul to God and help you fix your eyes on Him.
Then you are able to hope even when all hope appears
lost. R.C. Sproul says, "Hope is the ability to listen to
the music of the future. Faith is the courage to dance
to it in the present." So grab faith, pack it in your bags,
and enjoy your adventure with the Lord.

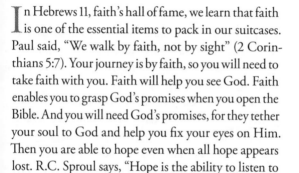

> *Lord, today I see the necessity of faith for my
> journey with You. Help me remember to
> always walk by faith, not by sight. Amen.*

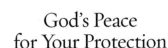

# God's Peace for Your Protection

Peace I leave with you; My peace I give to you;
not as the world gives do I give to you. Do not
let your heart be troubled, nor let it be fearful.

**JOHN 14:27**

---

Have you ever arrived at an airport, only to discover your flight was cancelled? Maybe you sat in the airport for hours before you even knew the revised schedule. How frustrating!

Sometimes your journey with God takes an unexpected turn. You encounter an obstacle in the road and need to wait for God's next step for you. What will help you when a barrier surprises you along the way? God's peace will protect you from the elements in life. His peace in your heart is unmoved by outward circumstances. Peace in the world depends on an absence of conflict or turmoil. You need God's peace whenever you are in trouble. Oh, how precious is the Lord's peace for your journey in life!

*Lord, thank You for Your peace in my heart, a
protection from worry in difficult times. Amen.*

# Courage That Makes You Unmovable

In the world you have tribulation, but take courage; I have overcome the world.

**JOHN 16:33**

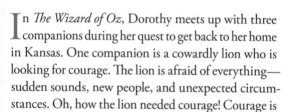

I n *The Wizard of Oz*, Dorothy meets up with three companions during her quest to get back to her home in Kansas. One companion is a cowardly lion who is looking for courage. The lion is afraid of everything—sudden sounds, new people, and unexpected circumstances. Oh, how the lion needed courage! Courage is the ability to be brave and stand up to the danger.

You too will need courage on your pilgrimage with the Lord. God promises that your travels will include tribulation. Difficulties threaten to press in on you and stir up fear and panic. When your world is threatened, remember that Jesus has overcome the world. Take your trouble to Jesus, rely on Him for strength and an overcoming attitude, and you will discover new courage to face your trial.

*Lord, thank You for Your courage. I rely on You today to help me be brave and stand up in the midst of troubles. Amen.*

# Joy for the Journey

Rejoice in the Lord always; again I will say, rejoice!

**PHILIPPIANS 4:4**

-----------------------------------

What does God say to you when you experience intense suffering and persecution? God wants to assure you that He knows the place of suffering. In fact, no one knows suffering like Jesus. He was crucified on the cross for you.

While imprisoned for the gospel, Paul wrote a letter to the suffering church at Philippi. Near the end of his letter, Paul arrived at the heart of his message for fellow sufferers: "Rejoice in the Lord always." Was he serious? Yes, for he had discovered the secret of joy in his own suffering. Joy is possible in suffering because of God's presence in your life. In your trial, when you draw near to the Lord, you will discover His joy in you. And you will discover what Nehemiah did: The joy of the Lord is your strength (Nehemiah 8:10). And then you will rejoice in the Lord.

*Lord, thank You for Your amazing joy—*
*my strength in trials. Amen.*

# Humility So You Can
# Make It Through

Clothe yourselves with humility toward
one another, for God is opposed to the
proud, but gives grace to the humble.

**1 PETER 5:5**

-------------------------

Humility is essential if you would embark on the pilgrimage of the heart. Humility enables you to love God and others. Peter encouraged suffering believers to wear humility like clothing. He describes humility as the one quality that ties together all the other virtues and brings an outpouring of God's grace. Humility always precedes exaltation. Someone has said, "He must take a low place before God, who would take a high place before men."

Humility entails a correct estimation of yourself. You are aware of God's greatness and your own smallness. Humility keeps you from trying to escape when God takes you through rough places on the journey. Sometimes you need to travel through a valley to get to the mountain. Humility will take you through to the other side.

*Lord, help me wear the clothing of humility*
*today on my pilgrimage of the heart. Amen.*

# Timing Is Everything

Rest in the LORD and wait patiently for Him...
Those who wait for the LORD, they
will inherit the land.

**PSALM 37:7,9**

-------------------------------

The boat was about to leave the dock. Two women climbed on board and looked for their tour guide. A closer look revealed that they were with the wrong tour! Thankfully, they were able to get off the boat before it sailed away. They ran back down the path and found their tour guide. What a relief! Just imagine if they'd persisted in going their own way instead of waiting for their leader. They would have missed part of the journey.

On your pilgrimage with God, He sometimes slows down the pace of your travel. You may feel as though you are sitting on a shelf, going nowhere. But God's timing is perfect. You need patience to wait on the Lord. Here's a good definition of *wait*: Watching Always, I Trust. Wait and watch to see what God will do today.

*Lord, I am waiting on You today, trusting
You to lead me on my journey. Amen.*

# Suffering for Doing What Is Right

If when you do what is right and suffer for it you patiently endure it, this finds favor with God.

**1 PETER 2:20**

-------------------------------------

Be assured, nice people don't always finish last. In this world, you may suffer for doing right, but ultimately you will reap a huge benefit. You receive God's favor. You will need endurance, which is the ability to bear things, not with passive resignation, but with blazing hope.

Endurance relies not on favorable circumstances, but on the presence of God. Endurance can prevail even if things become seemingly impossible. When you suffer for doing what is right, run to God and ask Him for endurance. You will be amazed how sweet your fellowship with God is when you endure unjust suffering. He is your dearest companion on the journey, and He will pour out unexpected blessings on you.

*Lord, You know the times when I've done what is right and suffered for it. I pray You will give me endurance to make it through to the other side. Amen.*

# Faithfulness to Serve the Lord

*He who is faithful in a very little
thing is faithful also in much.*

**LUKE 16:10**

---

Walter Henrichsen wrote a little book titled *Many Aspire—Few Attain*. Many people begin well but give up somewhere along the way. Some bright lights that shined brilliantly in the beginning have quickly burned out. Ministry excellence and influence can always be traced to faithfulness in the small things.

Never assess ministry opportunities with earthly eyes; instead, depend on the Lord's guidance. If He asks you to give water to someone who appears unimportant to you, pour your best cup of water in the name of the Lord. He may ask you to do many little things before He gives you something seemingly more important in ministry. Be faithful in the small things—making those phone calls, writing those e-mails, and maybe giving your best for the unknown person. Your faithfulness in the little things today will determine your faithfulness in much tomorrow. If you aspire now, find small ways to be faithful, and you will eventually attain.

*Lord, help me to follow You and be
faithful in everything I do. Amen.*

# Trust in the Lord

Trust in the LORD with all your heart
And do not lean on your own understanding.

**PROVERBS 3:5**

D o you find yourself second-guessing God's work
in your life? Do you look at every new occurrence
and form an immediate conclusion? If you think you
know God's purpose, you may actually be relying on
your own conclusions. If God doesn't take you where
you expect to go, you may become discouraged and
even fall into despair.

Cultivate trust in the Lord on your pilgrimage of
the heart. Trust in the Lord by leaning on God and His
Word. Real trust doesn't need to always understand.
In fact, when you are trusting in God, you realize you
can't possibly understand everything, for God's ways
are so much higher than our ways. Your trust acquires
a whimsical freedom when you are finally willing to
let go of complete understanding. Then God can take
you on the most unusual journeys and give you absolutely incredible views. Sometimes the very best views
require the most treacherous paths.

*Lord, I trust You today and let go of my
need to understand everything. Amen.*

# Mercy to Give
# God's Love Away

Be merciful, just as your Father is merciful.

**LUKE 6:36**

-----------------------------

On your journey, never forget the mercy of God. His compassion and tender love are like soothing salve for your painful wounds. His mercy can relieve your distress. God shows His mercy by showering you with blessings when you deserved nothing. God's mercy will prompt you to give His love away to undeserving people. You will find mercy welling up in your heart for friends and foes. Don't be afraid to act on an unusual idea of showing love for another. God may want to touch someone's life and use you as His instrument. God's mercy is always at work blessing needy, hurting hearts. When you reach out to others with God's mercy and love, you extend a lifeline to them. And as they draw closer to the Lord, you will too.

*Lord, today I ask that You will give me a*
*merciful heart and prompt me to reach*
*out to others with Your love. Amen.*

# Deepening Your Devotion

Let your heart therefore be wholly
devoted to the LORD our God.

**1 KINGS 8:61**

----

Deep devotion enables you to enjoy the fellowship and companionship of Jesus. It empowers you to seek Him and commune with Him wherever you are on your pilgrimage. Devotion is a committed and passionate loyalty to the King of your homeland, the kingdom of God. Your devotion to God is your concentrated effort and intention to see beyond the physical world to the spiritual realm. You feed and express your devotion by reading God's handbook, the Bible, so that you may know and understand His ways and character. When others watch you from a distance, they will notice that you are different from most in the world, for you have an undivided heart. You are fiercely loyal to your King. Today, think about the importance of devotion to God in your own life. Then ask yourself, *Is my heart wholly devoted to the Lord?*

*Lord, You are my King, and I look forward
to the day when I will live with You
forever in Your kingdom. Amen.*

# Traversing Life's Landscapes

God-traveled, these roads curve up the mountain,
and at the last turn—Zion! God in full view!

**PSALM 84:7 MSG**

---

When you travel to a region, you would do well to know the topography. Is it flat land or steep? Is it at sea level or a high elevation? The Bible gives you a glimpse of spiritual topography, especially in the psalms. You will discover mountaintops, wilderness, dry lands, green pastures, quiet waters, high places, and even the valley of the shadow of death.

When you familiarize yourself with the spiritual lay of the land, you will understand more clearly where God is leading you right now. No area of the journey is without purpose, for God is at work. You may be experiencing a mountain of change, a wilderness of searching, or a high place in God's glory. Those who travel with God always get to their destination.

*Lord, I need You more than ever, especially where*
*I am right now on our journey together. Amen.*

# When You Encounter Mountains of Change

Therefore we will not fear,
though the earth should change
and though the mountains slip
into the heart of the sea.

**PSALM 46:2**

---

Some people seem to thrive on unexpected changes. Others avoid change at all cost. Many changes are upsetting and uncomfortable. You encounter a bend in the road and wish you could take a more direct route.

But surprises, interruptions, and other changes test your priorities and affections. They remind you that this world won't lead you to the kingdom of God—you really are an alien in a foreign land. Dramatic changes will help you cast yourself more on God and find your home in Him. When you travel through mountains of change, you can always find great comfort in God's promises, for they will point you to a new hope in God. And hope will lead you through the mountain of change.

*Lord, I wouldn't have chosen this change, but You have led me here. I look to You for a promise in Your Word leading to a new hope in You. Amen.*

# Springs in the Valleys

He sends forth springs in the valleys.

**PSALM 104:10**

---

A re you in a valley right now? Be encouraged—God sends forth springs in the valleys. He sometimes reserves His most precious blessings for those in desperate places. Refreshing, living water from the Lord flows especially strong in the low places. God sometimes leads His servants into the valleys, where they are renewed by His springs. When others see you in the valley, they will wonder how you can possibly make it through. But you will experience the Lord's provision in your valley, and He will answer you Himself (Isaiah 41:17). Once you've taken a long, refreshing drink of the Lord's springs, your life will display God's renewal and restoration. When God sends His springs into your valley, He sends a profound message to everyone. Your life will speak of God's miraculous works (Isaiah 41:20). And then, perhaps others will also turn to God and surrender their lives to Him.

*Lord, thank You for Your renewing,*
*refreshing springs in the valleys. Amen.*

# Enjoying Green Pastures
# and Quiet Waters

He makes me lie down in green pastures;
He leads me beside quiet waters.

**PSALM 23:2**

---

A long the way on your pilgrimage, you will discover your need for comfort and contentment. The Lord is your Shepherd, and you are His sheep. You are under the care and concern of the Lord Himself. He promises to make you lie down in green pastures and lead you beside quiet waters.

Phillip Keller points out that a sheep will never lie down until it is free from fear, friction, torment, or hunger. Only the shepherd knows where to lead the sheep to water. Sheep don't find life-giving water by themselves; they need to follow their shepherd. When you enjoy green pastures and quiet waters by following your Lord, you discover true revival and restoration. Then you will know true contentment, the experience of having enough. Follow the lead of your Shepherd today and enjoy true heart renewal.

*Lord, thank You for leading me, Your sheep, to*
*green pastures and quiet waters. Amen.*

# The High Places of God

The Lord God is my strength,
And He has made my feet like hinds' feet,
And makes me walk on my high places.

**HABAKKUK 3:19**

Oh, what a day it is when the Lord leads you to the high places, where you experience pure delight in God Himself. You will love this place. In the high places, God reveals Himself in new ways to you, His pilgrim. You may enjoy the high places of God even in a prison experience. John Bunyan did. Corrie ten Boom did. Paul did. Habakkuk, a prophet who lived during a devastating time in the history of Israel, discovered that though he lost everything, he could still rejoice in the Lord and find the high places with God.

Though your life seems to be at its lowest point, you can enjoy God's presence. Worship and praise Him today. When you rejoice, God gives you a heart of adoration and leads you up the path to His high places, where you will see a magnificent vision of your Lord.

*Lord, take me to Your high places today. Amen.*

# FAITH

# Great Faith

O woman, your faith is great; it shall
be done for you as you wish.

**MATTHEW 15:28**

A woman, desperate and brokenhearted because of her suffering daughter, fell at Jesus' feet. She cried, "Lord, help me!" Jesus did not immediately answer her. His delay only moved her to a deeper faith, and she pressed Him for an answer in her trouble. Jesus admired her persistent belief and replied, "O woman, your faith is great; it shall be done for you as you wish."

Wouldn't you love to hear Jesus say to you, "Your faith is great"? What do you need from Jesus today? Ask the Lord to give you a deep realization of your need for Him, a knowledge of His promises in His Word, a new courage to run to Him for help, and patience to wait for His answer. Then perhaps you too will hear those words, "O woman, your faith is great."

*Lord, I lay all my burdens and requests before*
*You now and look to You with an expectant faith,*
*waiting for Your amazing answer. Amen.*

# What Is Faith?

*Just say the word, and my servant will be healed.*

**LUKE 7:7**

---

A centurion with a dying servant sent Jesus an outrageous request. He understood Jesus' authority and knew His word was enough to accomplish mighty miracles. So he told Jesus not to come any closer, for he was not worthy. "Just say the word, and my servant will be healed."

Do you see the secret to faith? God's Word possesses the authority to command your belief and actions. If God says it, you can launch out in faith and take Him at His Word. Faith is taking God at His Word. Today, open the pages of your Bible, grab a powerful promise, take Him at His Word, and trust Him with your life. When you live by faith, perhaps Jesus will marvel at you as He did the centurion and say, "Not even in Israel have I found such great faith."

*Lord, help me take You at Your Word, believing what You say more than what I see or feel. Amen.*

# Even Small Faith
# Can Be Enough

If you have faith the size of a mustard
seed…nothing will be impossible to you.

**MATTHEW 17:20**

------------------------------

D o you feel as though you will never have a great
faith? Do you think your faith is hardly able to
deal with the difficulties of the day and certainly not
enough to move a mountain? Even a small faith is
enough when placed in a great God. The quality of your
faith counts more than the quantity. Jesus said that even
mustard-seed-sized faith moves mountains. Nothing is
impossible for the one with mustard-seed faith.

Imagine a tiny seed resting in the palm of your
hand. You can hardly even see it. That's your faith. And
yet your mustard-seed faith, placed in a great God who
can do the impossible, results in more than you can ask
or imagine. So today, focus your tiny faith on God and
His Word, believe Him in the midst of your great need,
and watch mountains move in your life.

*Lord, my faith is small, but You are infinite.*
*Move mountains in my life today. Amen.*

# Looking Down from the Top

We don't look at the troubles we can
see now; rather, we fix our gaze on
things that cannot be seen.

**2 CORINTHIANS 4:18 NLT**

-------

Faith dwells on eternal, unseen truths from God's
Word instead of focusing on temporal troubles that
try the soul. When you exercise your faith by taking
God at His Word, you will enjoy His eternal perspective. The eternal perspective is the ability to see all of life
from God's point of view and apply that new view to
your present life. Instead of wallowing in the darkness
of your troubles, you gaze from above, gaining the eternal view of your life. You look down from the top.

Hannah Whitall Smith explains, "Trials assume
a very different aspect when looked down upon from
above." Where is your focus today? Ask God to help
you look at life from above and give you His eternal
perspective.

*Lord, will You take me to the mountaintop today
and give me Your view of my circumstance? Help
me to see life from Your eternal perspective. Amen.*

# The Spy of the Soul

Then the LORD spoke to Moses saying, "Send
out for yourself men so that they may
spy out the land of Canaan, which I am
going to give to the sons of Israel."

**NUMBERS 13:1-2**

One day, some leaders of God's people were commissioned as the Lord's spies, privileged to gain a first look at God's Promised Land. They discovered God's promise was true—the land was indeed flowing with milk and honey. But their view was obscured by seemingly overwhelming obstacles. Most of the spies became afraid of the strength of the people in the land and the fortified cities. Joshua and Caleb alone believed God's promise.

Octavius Winslow says, "Faith is the spiritual spy of the soul. It travels far into the promised land and gathers the ripe clusters—the evidences and earnest of its reality and richness." Open God's Word today and exercise your faith as a spiritual spy in the fruitful, abundant land of God's promises.

*Lord, open my eyes today and help me*
*see beyond my troubles to the beauty and*
*power of Your promises. Amen.*

# It's a Real Test

When troubles come your way, consider
it an opportunity for great joy. For you
know that when your faith is tested, your
endurance has a chance to grow.

**JAMES 1:2-3 NLT**

Have you been thinking lately, *Why is this trouble in my life?* In God's economy, trials test your faith, and this process transforms you and makes you stronger than you were before. Every trouble you face is a faith test, proving your genuine faith, strengthening your ability to believe God, and giving you endurance in life.

Why are some people able to make it through spiritual tests with boundless courage and triumph? They grasp the promise of God and hold on to it like a tether of the soul linked to God's mighty power. The test proves their faith is genuine and expands faith's ability to trust God. Stand firm today, realizing that the testing of your faith is making you strong in the kingdom of God.

*Lord, help me stand strong in the testing of
my faith and pass with flying colors as I trust
You when troubles come my way. Amen.*

# The Most Sublime Utterance of Faith

Though He slay me, yet I will trust Him.

**JOB 13:15 NKJV**

------------------------------

Some have called their most painful trial in life a "dark night of the soul." Job plummeted into the dark night when he thought he would lose his life. Even in your dark night, you can hold on and press through to a new expression of faith. Job discovered a new faith when he cried out, "Though He slay me, yet I will trust Him."

Oswald Chambers says, "Faith in the Bible is faith in God against everything that contradicts Him—I will remain true to God's character whatever He may do. 'Though He slay me, yet will I trust Him'—this is the most sublime utterance of faith in the whole of the Bible." Today, remain true to God, hold on to His Word, and move to a new expression of faith where you can say, "Even in this, Lord, I will trust You."

*Lord, regardless of what I face today, I trust*
*You. Give me a great faith in You. Amen.*

# He Knows

He knows the way I take.

**JOB 23:10**

---

The testing of your faith is a personal and solitary life experience. No one can truly know or understand your pain except you and God. The psalmist assures us that the Lord is near the brokenhearted and saves those who are crushed in spirit (Psalm 34:18). Because God is near when you are broken and crushed, you can enjoy Him in deeper ways during those times. Peter explained that in your fiery ordeal, you "share in the sufferings of Christ" (1 Peter 4:13). Paul even felt privileged to experience trials in his walk with Christ because they led to the intimate "fellowship of His sufferings" (Philippians 3:10).

The fact that God knows was a tremendous encouragement to Job, and God's awareness of your deep suffering will provide tremendous solace for your hurting heart as well. One never invites suffering, but when it comes your way, you can know that you aren't alone. He knows.

*Lord, thank You for the encouragement today that
You know the way I take. I am staying near You
and look to You for comfort and strength. Amen.*

# Gold Faith

*When He has tried me, I shall come forth as gold.*

**JOB 23:10**

---

T he refining of precious metals is an extensive process. As far back as 550 BC, refiners would heat the fire to 1700 degrees, melt the silver or gold, and pour it into clay jars. Impurities would float to the top. The refiner knew the metal was pure when he could see his perfect reflection. The purity of the metal turned it into a valuable treasure.

According to Peter, the testing of your faith is more precious than gold. God has a purpose and goal in mind when He refines your faith. Once the fire reveals your genuine faith, the ordeal will bring praise, honor, and glory at the unveiling of Jesus Christ (1 Peter 1:7).

Job found courage by reminding himself of God's purpose for his trial, and you can do the same in your difficult times. Just think about the gold! That's what your faith is producing—the pure gold of godly character, the reflection of Christ in you, and life that lasts forever.

*Lord, thank You that when You have tried me, I will come forth as gold. Amen.*

# Going for the Gold

This is the victory that has overcome
the world—our faith.

**1 JOHN 5:4**

---

In the Olympic Games, athletes compete against each other for the gold medal. Our adversaries, however, are greater than even world-class athletes. Paul said we struggle against "the world forces of this darkness" (Ephesians 6:12). John simply calls them "the world." These forces attempt to lure us away from Christ through godless thinking, life without convictions, self-sufficiency, acquiring money, pursuing possessions, and achieving success. You must "fight the good fight of faith" (1 Timothy 6:12) against these influences.

Oswald Chambers said that faith is a fight "always, not sometimes." Faith will give you victory. Every time you take a step of faith, you are gaining a victory and winning the gold. Yes, living by faith is a fight at times. Your feelings or circumstances will try to keep you from taking God at His Word. Press through—fight the fight of faith and gain the victory.

*Lord, help me fight the fight of faith today by
living for You and taking You at Your word. Give
me victory by strengthening my faith. Amen.*

# Fix Your Eyes on Jesus

Let us run with endurance the race that is set
before us, fixing our eyes on Jesus,
the author and perfecter of faith.

**HEBREWS 12:1-2**

Life is like an endurance race that lasts until you cross the finish line and step from time into eternity. Someday, you will stand face-to-face with Jesus, the author and perfecter of your faith. Imagine Him looking at you and seeing His completed work in you. What a day of celebration! Prepare for that day by fixing your eyes on Jesus now.

When you endure hardship, fixing your eyes on Jesus will give you the strength and courage to overcome the world (John 16:33). When you are wronged, fixing your eyes on Jesus will enable you to forgive. When you experience losses, fixing your eyes on Jesus will comfort your heart. The more you look at Him, the stronger your faith will become. Today, in whatever you experience, fix your eyes on Jesus.

*Lord, remind me today to fix my eyes on You. Amen.*

# No Wasted Glories

Be still, and know that I am God.

**PSALM 46:10 NIV**

---

God invites you to an intimate relationship, a first-hand experience of Him in your daily life. When God says, "Be still, and know that I am God," He is inviting you to take a step of faith, open the pages of His Word, and know Him. How will you respond to God's invitation? What will you do with God's Word, filled as it is with truth after truth of God's wondrous nature and attributes? When you stand face-to-face with your Lord, you'll want to know that you have known Him. Imagine your confidence in His presence, having no wasted glories. You made the most of His revelation, opening the pages of the Bible day by day and poring over all He said, just so you could know Him more.

No wasted glories, dear friend. Will you draw near and know your God today?

*O Lord, I want to know You for myself. When I open the pages of the Bible, cause my eyes to see and taste Your glory. Amen.*

# God's Multimedia

The heavens are telling of the glory of God;
And their expanse is declaring
the work of His hands.

**PSALM 19:1**

H ave you ever visited an art gallery and looked at the intricate details of the paintings on display? The longer you look at a masterpiece, the more you see.

In the same way, your knowledge of God grows as you carefully consider His creation. Stop and contemplate the details of His beautiful masterpiece, His multimedia revelation. Gaze at the lines in a leaf, the color of a flower, the rushing water of a stream, or the expanse of the stars at night. You will never be disappointed in your discoveries when you linger long at the sermons of creation. Today, take some time to notice God's handiwork. When you meditate on His works, your faith will grow.

*Lord, thank You for giving us a multimedia
view of who You are through Your creation.
Give me eyes to notice Your glory and the
wisdom to apply it to my life. Amen.*

# God's Great Heart

How often I wanted to gather your children
together, the way a hen gathers her chicks
under her wings, and you were unwilling.

**MATTHEW 23:37**

Sometimes we can feel as if God is distant and our feet are bound to the earth. But this is our view of things, not God's. God is thinking about you even now and longing to draw you close. Jesus explained God's heart when He said, "How often I wanted to gather your children together, the way a hen gathers her chicks under her wings." Notice the word *often*, and you will realize that God *always* wants you near Him, safe in His arms.

Today, by faith, will you stop and hear the heart of your God? He loves you. He is not coy; in fact, He wears His heart on His sleeve! He is holding out His arms all day, waiting for you to draw near.

*Lord, I draw near today into Your open arms,*
*willing to be close, to be safe in Your care. Amen.*

# God's Vocabulary

That which is highly esteemed among
men is detestable in the sight of God.

**LUKE 16:15**

-------------------------------------

H ave you ever looked up a word in a dictionary and discovered your definition was not even close to the true meaning? Reading the Bible sometimes works the same way. It provides a glimpse into God's spiritual realm and reveals His point of view. We discover immediately that the world's thinking (and sometimes our own!) is upside-down. People who are great in the world may be small in God's economy. The wisdom of the world is foolishness to God. And worldly wealth may lead us into poverty in God's economy. We need to learn God's vocabulary and His definitions so we don't suffer from the malady of upside-down thinking.

Today, ask yourself, *Do I share God's heart and look at the world from His perspective or my own earthly view?* Then open the pages of the Bible and see as God sees, think as He thinks, and love as He loves.

> *Lord, thank You for the mighty gift of Your
> Word. Help me view the world from Your
> eyes and learn Your vocabulary. Amen.*

# When I Feel Weak

When I am weak, then I am strong.

**2 CORINTHIANS 12:10**

God will often ask you to act beyond your own natural capabilities. He never intends for you to rely on yourself. He wants to be strong in you through the power of the Holy Spirit. The weaker you are, the stronger He can be in you. When you are weak, rest assured that God is about to display His great power in your life.

Paul realized his weakness was the very platform of God's power and strength. He was able to say, "When I am weak, then I am strong" and "I can do all things through Him who strengthens me" (Philippians 4:13). If you feel as though you are facing an impossible task, learn to say, "I can't, but He can." Then launch out in faith and watch God empower you with His strength.

*O Lord, I realize my weakness and inability*
*to accomplish all of today's tasks and fulfill*
*all my responsibilities. Thank You for giving*
*me Your strength and power. Amen.*

# Radical Faith

We walk by faith, not by sight.

**2 CORINTHIANS 5:7**

-----------------------------

Genuine faith is radical. With eyes of faith, we can see things that are invisible. Our physical eyes rarely give us the whole picture, but when we walk by faith, we perceive what is eternal and true.

Sometimes life is very much like the facade of a movie set. What you thought was true and permanent may only be temporary. What God says in His Word is the truth. You can take God at His Word, build your life on His truths, and count on the firm foundation of His promises. If some days you don't feel loved, rely on God's Word: "I have loved you with an everlasting love" (Jeremiah 31:3). When you feel as though life is over, count on God's promise of a future and a hope (Jeremiah 29:11). Resolve today to get radical and walk by faith, not by sight.

*Lord, thank You for giving me the firm foundation of Your Word. Help me walk by faith, not by sight. Amen.*

# Growing Strong in Faith

Faith comes from hearing, and
hearing by the word of Christ.

**ROMANS 10:17**

How can you grow strong in your faith? Paul gives us the answer in today's verse. Your faith becomes strong when you spend time alone with God in His Word. The secret to great faith is dedicating time in your day to God and His Word. Slow down to hear Him speak. Read a verse in the Bible and stop to think about what God is saying. Look for significant words, phrases, and verses when you read a chapter in God's Word. Write your most important insights in your journal or quiet time notebook.

When you slow down with God and read His Word, you will be amazed at how much you notice. Today, live in God's Word and watch your faith grow.

*Lord, help me slow down, faithfully open*
*Your Word, and live in it long enough to*
*hear what You have to say to me. Amen.*

# Shipwrecked or Shored Up?

Some have made shipwreck of their faith.

**1 TIMOTHY 1:19 ESV**

Today you will make some choices that will either fortify your faith or weaken it. When you live in God's Word, you shore up your faith, strengthening your heart to meet the challenges of the day. When your Bible remains closed, sitting on the shelf, you are in danger of being shipwrecked or washed out to sea with the next storm.

Paul encouraged his disciple Timothy to be fearless in his struggle, keeping a firm grip on his faith. Always remember that a Bible in the hand is worth two in the bookcase. So grab your Bible today, read its words, and write out your most significant insights in your journal or notebook. Then carry what God says in your heart and live it out in your life.

*Lord, I desire to have a strong, shored-up faith, not a shipwrecked faith. Help me open the pages of Your Word, listen to You speak, and live by what You say. Amen.*

# More Than You Can Imagine

Now to Him who is able to do far more abundantly
beyond all that we ask or think…to Him be the glory.

**EPHESIANS 3:20**

Darlene Diebler Rose, a missionary, was taken captive and placed in a concentration camp during World War II. One day, gazing out her prison window, she saw someone quickly give one of the prisoners a clump of bananas. Darlene's starvation led her to near madness thinking about those bananas. *Lord, if only I could have one banana!* Then she reasoned, *How could God give me a banana?* Darlene wrestled with the power and sufficiency of God but continued to believe in His promises. One day she heard footsteps approaching her cell. She watched a hand reach in, and throw onto the floor of her cell the unimaginable and unbelievable answer to her prayers. Bananas—not just one, but 92 bananas!

What's your need today, dear friend? God can do more than you can ask or imagine.

*Lord, I bring my need to You today. I can't
wait to see You do more than I ask or imagine
according to Your power. Amen.*

# Forever Faithful

Be faithful until death.

**REVELATION 2:10**

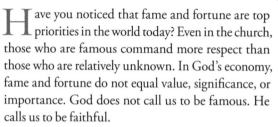

Have you noticed that fame and fortune are top priorities in the world today? Even in the church, those who are famous command more respect than those who are relatively unknown. In God's economy, fame and fortune do not equal value, significance, or importance. God does not call us to be famous. He calls us to be faithful.

When you are faithful, you are reliable. You trust in God's promise. God can count on you to carry out His assignments. And He can also rely on you to trust what He says in His Word. A faithful follower of Christ knows God's Word, embraces His promises, and rests on those promises even in the midst of a challenging circumstance.

Today, will you be faithful even in the small thing, whatever it may be? For when you are faithful in little, you will be faithful in much.

*Lord, help me to be faithful in every assignment.*
*Help me know Your promises and trust them*
*in every challenging circumstance. Amen.*

# Your Great Reward

I will give you the crown of life.

**REVELATION 2:10**

---

One of the highlights in every Olympic competition is the awards ceremony. Similarly, one of the highlights of your life will be the heavenly reward ceremony, where you will receive the crown of life. You will experience the joy of your Master and hear these words from Jesus: "Well done, good and faithful servant." Imagine the wonder of that moment, when you look in the eyes of your Lord. Then you will know that your faithfulness, even in the fiery trial, was worth every enduring effort.

Today, do you long to be faithful? Are you in the heat of a fiery trial? Find a promise in God's Word and trust what He says in the heat of your trouble. As you do, your faithful God will empower you to be even more faithful—more like Him.

*Lord, I so long to receive the crown of life*
*and hear Your words, "Well done, good and*
*faithful servant." Help me draw near and fill*
*me with a new faithfulness today. Amen.*

LOVE

# Everlasting Love

I have loved you with an everlasting love;
Therefore I have drawn you with lovingkindness.

**JEREMIAH 31:3**

In an ever-changing world, you can count on one unchanging truth: God loves you with an everlasting love. Perhaps you feel as though everything in your life is falling apart. God's love can be your comfort today. He surrounds you with His infinite compassion and kindness. Even if you feel lost and abandoned, you can rest assured that God's love will find you.

Author J. Vernon McGee once asked a little boy, "How long is everlasting?"

The boy responded, "I reckon it's a pretty long time."

And so it is. God's love outlasts all adversity, all sin, all obstacles, and all human relationships. Today, think about God's eternal love. Draw near to your Lord and rejoice in the fact that everything on earth may change, but God and His love last forever.

*Lord, thank You for Your everlasting love for
me. In the changes I am enduring today, help
me focus on Your amazing love. Amen.*

# The Power of God's Love

God is love, and the one who abides in love
abides in God, and God abides in him.

**1 JOHN 4:16**

-------------------------------------

God's love is higher and greater than the conditional love you see in the world. People love conditionally when they say, "I love you because you do this or that" or "I love you because you're so beautiful." God's love is unconditional and depends only on Him, not on you. Your performance or appearance can't make Him love you more than He loves you now. God's essential nature is unconditional love. John said, "God *is* love." God's love imparts value and worth to you. God prizes you so much that He gave His beloved Son on your behalf. Think deeply about the power of God's unconditional love for you and experience a new freedom to draw near to God, live for Him, and love others.

*Lord, thank You for loving me. I can't earn*
*Your love, but I can receive and experience it*
*today in each waking moment. Amen.*

# The Greatest Realization

Christ's love is greater than anyone can know.

**EPHESIANS 3:19 NCV**

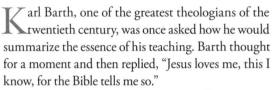

Karl Barth, one of the greatest theologians of the twentieth century, was once asked how he would summarize the essence of his teaching. Barth thought for a moment and then replied, "Jesus loves me, this I know, for the Bible tells me so."

Like Barth, you may have a great intellect. But the greatest truth you can reflect on is that Christ loved you enough to lay down His life for you. In turbulent times, clouds of doubt can limit your spiritual vision, and you may begin to question Christ's love. When this happens, turn your gaze to the cross. Someone once said, "It wasn't the nails that held Him to the cross, but His love for you."

Watch Christ set His course for Jerusalem, knowing that incomprehensible suffering awaited Him there. He sacrificed His life to give you eternal life. His love is truly greater than anyone can know.

*Lord, thank You for Your great love for me—greater than I can comprehend. Thank You for dying on the cross for me that I might live with You forever. Amen.*

# Effective Love

God so loved the world, that He
gave His only begotten Son.

**JOHN 3:16**

------------------------------------

Once upon a time, a man stumbled into a bed of quicksand. Four men passed by, each offering his perspective on the poor man's predicament. The first one said, "You shouldn't have gotten in there in the first place." The second one said, "This will be a good lesson for anyone else who comes along." The third man said, "This must have been God's will." But the fourth man spread himself on solid ground, reached out to the desperate man, and said, "Take my hand. I can pull you out."

God, in His love, sees your need and does something about it. He may not always give you what you want, but He will always give you what you need. He provided for your sin through Jesus' death on the cross. Because He loves you, you can know that He will provide everything you need—today, tomorrow, and always.

*Lord, thank You for Your love. You don't just talk about love; You express love, giving me abundant daily provision. Thank You, Lord. Amen.*

# The Proof of God's Amazing Love

*The proof of God's amazing love is this:*
*that it was while we were sinners*
*that Christ died for us.*

**ROMANS 5:8 PHILLIPS**

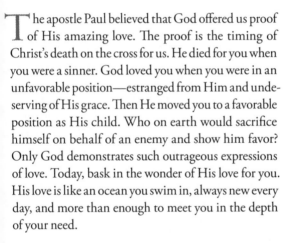

The apostle Paul believed that God offered us proof of His amazing love. The proof is the timing of Christ's death on the cross for us. He died for you when you were a sinner. God loved you when you were in an unfavorable position—estranged from Him and undeserving of His grace. Then He moved you to a favorable position as His child. Who on earth would sacrifice himself on behalf of an enemy and show him favor? Only God demonstrates such outrageous expressions of love. Today, bask in the wonder of His love for you. His love is like an ocean you swim in, always new every day, and more than enough to meet you in the depth of your need.

*Lord, thank You for the proof of Your amazing love.*
*Help me realize Your great love in my life today. Amen.*

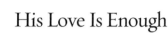

# His Love Is Enough

For if while we were enemies we were
reconciled to God through the death
of His Son, much more, having been
reconciled, we shall be saved by His life.

**ROMANS 5:10**

---

Charles Wesley grew up in a religious home, stud-
ied at Oxford University, and served as a missionary. In spite of his training, he knew very little joy or
peace in his own heart. After a discouraging time in
America, he met with a group of Moravian Christians
in London. Wesley learned he could do nothing to earn
his own salvation, and he was saved by grace through
faith alone. He wrote in his journal, "At midnight I
gave myself to Christ, assured that I was safe, whether
sleeping or waking."

Do you ever wonder if your sin is too much for God
to forgive, if it's beyond the power of His love? Always
remember that He reconciled you to Himself while you
were an enemy. If His love was enough then, surely His
love is enough for you now.

*Lord, thank You that Your love is more*
*than enough for me. Amen.*

# Hold Your Head High

We may hold our heads high in the light of God's
love because of the reconciliation Christ has made.

**ROMANS 5:11 PHILLIPS**

---

When you survey the wondrous cross of Christ and realize all He has accomplished for you, what is your response? You can hold your head high in the light of His love. Even if your finances fail, you have no job, or you lose your home, one bright hope remains. God loves you. Because of His love, you can move beyond the despair of the world into a shining hope.

Corrie ten Boom was able to hold her head high in the darkness of a cruel concentration camp. She was empowered to say, "With Christ, even if the worst happens, the best remains. And His light is brighter than the deepest darkness." Regardless of what happens today, hold your head high and remember that nothing can separate you from God's love (Romans 8:38-39).

*Lord, help me hold my head high in
the light of Your love. Amen.*

# Your Claim to Fame

One of the disciples, the one Jesus loved dearly,
was reclining against him, his head on his shoulder.

**JOHN 13:23 MSG**

When you think about your life, what is your claim to fame? What defines your life? When people think of you, what will come to their mind? George Washington will always be remembered as the first president of the United States of America. Mickey Mantle will always be known as a great baseball player. When you think of Michelangelo, you think of the Sistine Chapel.

The apostle John referred to himself as "the one Jesus loved dearly." John was not arrogantly saying Jesus loved him more than all the other disciples. He was humbly explaining, without even mentioning his own name, that he knew and experienced the love of Christ. Christ's love meant so much to him that every other life experience paled in comparison. May you make the same claim to fame: "I am the one Jesus loved dearly."

*Lord, thank You that even I can experience Your amazing love. Your love is my claim to fame. Amen.*

# There's Always
# Room for One More

One of the disciples, the one Jesus loved dearly,
was reclining against him, his head on his shoulder.

**JOHN 13:23 MSG**

-------------------------

Why could John claim he was the one Jesus loved?
John may have experienced Jesus' love in greater
measure than others, for he reclined next to Christ and
rested his head on His shoulder. John boldly drew near
to Christ and was rewarded with an intimate relationship with the King. Perhaps he enjoyed a richer experience of Christ's love because he was willing to lean in
and know Him more.

There's always room for one more in Christ's embrace. He invites you to come to Him (Matthew 11:28-
30) and enjoy rich fellowship (Revelation 3:20). If you
want to be like John—one whom Jesus loves dearly—
get close to Jesus and live in constant communion with
Him. Then you will know what John knew—the un-
fathomable love of Jesus Christ.

*Lord, I want to know Your love as John did*
*and lean in to Your embrace today. Amen.*

# Will You Dance?

I have found David the son of Jesse, a man
after My heart, who will do all My will.

**ACTS 13:22**

---

The Lord is looking for people who will dance with
Him, following His lead and enjoying His embrace.
He found one man who was just the right kind of
dancer. David, the man after God's own heart, loved
God, shared His heart, followed His lead, and moved
in perfect precision as he danced with Him. God evidently loved dancing with David! In fact, He told others about their dance.

Imagine hearing God say this about you: "I have
found her to be a woman after My heart, who will do
all My will." The Lord is always looking for dancers.
Will you dance with Him? If so, then surrender everything that keeps you from leaning into His embrace.
And then, dear friend, just dance!

*Lord, today I say yes to dancing with You. Help
me lean into your embrace and follow Your lead
as I learn from You in Your Word. Amen.*

# The Sweet Aroma of His Love

> God leads us from place to place in one
> perpetual victory parade. Through us, he
> brings knowledge of Christ. Everywhere we
> go, people breathe in the exquisite fragrance.

**2 CORINTHIANS 2:14-15 MSG**

-------------------------------

When you know Christ, your life tells an amazing story of Christ's love. The story is sweet, bringing a fragrance to others when they come to know Christ. What is your story? Think about how you first discovered Christ's love for you. You may have an amazing story of transformation. Or you may have known Christ from a young age. As you share the exquisite fragrance of your life with others, it will draw them to Christ and His life-changing love.

Write out your story and share it with all who will listen. People will be encouraged when you explain how your mess became His message, your tests became His testimony, and your history became His story.

*Lord, open the door today for me to talk about*
*what You have done in my life with someone*
*who needs to hear about Your love. Amen.*

# The Gift of His Love

We love because He first loved us.

**1 JOHN 4:19**

---

Corrie ten Boom watched the balding, heavyset man in a gray overcoat move slowly toward her from the back of the church. In a flash, she remembered him from Ravensbruck, the concentration camp where she and so many others had suffered. He was the guard who cruelly mistreated her beloved sister, Betsie.

But Corrie saw him now with outstretched hand. "Fraulein, will you forgive me?"

In those next moments, Corrie wrestled. She knew she must forgive, but how could she? The Holy Spirit, faithful as always, reminded her of God's promise, "The love of God has been poured out within our hearts through the Holy Spirit who was given to us" (Romans 5:5). By faith, Corrie extended her hand, and as she did, she was filled with overwhelming love and forgiveness.

Who needs God's love in your life today? Ask God to fill you with His love, knowing you can love because He has first loved you.

*Lord, help me reach out to others who need*
*Your love and forgiveness today. Amen.*

# The Priority of God

*You shall love the LORD your God with all your heart,*
*and with all your soul, and with all your mind.*

**MATTHEW 22:37**

---

Looking for a way to test Jesus and catch Him in a fundamental error, the Pharisees asked Him, "Teacher, which is the great commandment in the Law?" (Matthew 22:36). But Jesus understood the meaning of the Scriptures much better than the religious experts did. After all, He is the Word of God (John 1:1). Jesus answered them immediately because He is God and knew what to say. He turned the tables on the Pharisees, for their question brought out a fundamental teaching.

Jesus forever defined the primary focus and priority for all His followers: loving God. Loving God is at the heart of everything you do in life. Your relationships, your spiritual condition, and your ministry flow from your love relationship with the Lord. Focus on loving the Lord and watch your life flourish as you reap the fruitful results of following the Lord's great commandment.

*Lord, I choose today to love You with all*
*my heart and soul and mind. Amen.*

# From Trial to Triumph

Once you have turned again,
strengthen your brothers.

**LUKE 22:32**

---

Where can you find encouragement when you've failed and your life seems to be falling apart? Peter, the disciple who denied Christ three times, walked a path of failure, discouragement, and disappointment. Jesus told Peter in advance that He had prayed for him that his faith would not fail. His encouragement continued, for He saw beyond the trial to the triumph. "Once you have turned again, strengthen your brothers."

Jesus has a plan for your life, and nothing can thwart His plan for you. Even Peter's three denials did not disqualify him from ministry. In fact, he was promoted to leader of the first-century church. Maybe you feel as though your life is ruined because of your failures. Jesus sees beyond your trial to your triumph. His love and forgiveness will lead you to a new, spacious place of grace and glory.

*Lord, thank You for Your forgiveness in my*
*failures and Your triumphs in my trials. Amen.*

# He Remembers You

Even these may forget, but I will not forget you.

**ISAIAH 49:15**

---

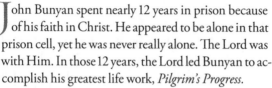

John Bunyan spent nearly 12 years in prison because of his faith in Christ. He appeared to be alone in that prison cell, yet he was never really alone. The Lord was with Him. In those 12 years, the Lord led Bunyan to accomplish his greatest life work, *Pilgrim's Progress.*

Maybe you are in a prison of sorts in an obscure corner of the world, feeling as though everyone has forgotten you. You can know God never forgets you, but always remembers you (Genesis 8:1). When God remembers you, He pays special attention to you and pours out His favor. When God remembered Noah, the floodwaters receded, and God brought him to dry land. Whatever you face today, know that God remembers you. And in this season of feeling alone, perhaps you will accomplish your greatest work, just as Bunyan accomplished his.

*Lord, I have known the feeling of aloneness. I take comfort in the fact that You never forget me, but rather always remember me. Amen.*

# Written on His Hands

I have inscribed you on the palms of My hands;
Your walls are continually before Me.

**ISAIAH 49:16**

Do you ever doubt your importance to God? Sometimes, especially in the most difficult trials, God may seem so distant that you wonder if He realizes you are in trouble. In Isaiah's time, the people of Israel felt abandoned by God, and they accused Him of forsaking them. God said they were so precious to Him that they were inscribed on His hands.

If you are inscribed on the palms of His hands, you are always in His presence. God is present with you, and you are present with Him. There is never a moment when you are not on His mind and heart. Others may quickly forget you, but God will never let you out of His sight or stop thinking about you.

*Lord, thank You that I am inscribed on the*
*palms of Your hands. You are always with*
*me, and I am always with You. Knowing You*
*love me is my great comfort today. Amen.*

# New Every Morning

The LORD's lovingkindnesses indeed never cease,
For His compassions never fail.
They are new every morning.

**LAMENTATIONS 3:22-23**

------------------------------

Every morning, you can count on the sun's glistening rays to brighten the day. Jeremiah, the weeping prophet, discovered a ray of hope in his trial. He found comfort knowing that God's loving-kindnesses make new appearances in his life every morning. David poured out his prayers before God in the morning and then eagerly watched (Psalm 5:3). Why was David so eager to watch and wait after talking with God? He had discovered God's amazing response.

Even in great trouble you can look forward to new expressions of God's love, kindness, and compassion. Just when you think life may be over, God surprises you with unexpected answers. You may receive an encouraging phone call or a word of comfort from a verse in the Bible. Look expectantly each morning and keep your eyes open for God's love. His compassionate heart can't help but pour out blessings on His children. He promises.

*Lord, thank You for the amazing promise*
*that Your loving-kindnesses and compassions*
*are new every morning. Amen.*

# Chosen and Beloved

So, as those who have been chosen of God, holy
and beloved, put on a heart of compassion.

**COLOSSIANS 3:12**

-----------------------------

Think back for a moment to your elementary-school days. In PE class, or maybe during recess, did you watch nervously as captains picked people to be on their teams? Do you remember desperately wanting to be chosen? If you were the last one picked, you probably felt awful. But if a captain freely chose you, you likely felt special.

God wants you to know He chooses you. When He selects you, He makes you beautiful. He cleanses you from all unrighteousness and makes you holy and righteous. God loves you with an affectionate love. He calls you *beloved*, meaning that He values you. You are precious to Him. He treasures you. Maybe you have experienced a devastating rejection or an unkind word from someone. Knowing you are God's treasure changes the landscape of your life. Revel in His love. Swim in it. Immerse yourself in the knowledge that God loves you beyond measure.

*Lord, help me focus on Your love for me,*
*especially when I feel alone in the world. Thank*
*You that I am Your beloved. Amen.*

# Precious in His Sight

Since you were precious in My sight,
You have been honored,
and I have loved you.

**ISAIAH 43:4 NKJV**

G old is a precious metal. Diamonds are precious gems. Did you know that you are precious to God? He values you as one of His greatest treasures. You are worth more to God than the costliest gem. He proved your value by sending His own beloved Son to die on the cross for you. Just think how precious you are to God.

Have you ever looked into the face of a newborn child and discovered an overwhelming desire to hold that baby close so nothing could ever harm it? The affectionate love welled up in your heart because you regarded that child as precious. Your heavenly Father holds you close, for you are precious to Him. Rejoice today in how important you are to your God.

*Lord, I find great joy in knowing I am
precious to You. Help me appreciate and
love You with all my heart today. Amen.*

# The Apple of His Eye

He who touches you, touches the apple of His eye.

**ZECHARIAH 2:8**

---

God is extremely protective of His people, watching over every detail of their lives. He sees each one as the apple of His eye. The apple of the eye refers to the pupil, the part of the eye through which light passes. God warns His enemies, through Zechariah, of the folly of trying to harm His people, for they are the apple of His eye. God jealously watches over His people as one would protect the most sensitive part of the eye. If an object comes toward your face, you instinctively raise your arms to protect your eyes. So too, God is always present, watching over His precious people. And any who would want to harm God's people are coming against God's beloved treasure. Ultimately, He will bring you, the apple of His eye, safely home to be with Him forever in His kingdom.

*Lord, thank You for watching over me*
*as the apple of Your eye. Amen.*

# He Cares For You

Cast all your anxiety on him
because he cares for you.

**1 PETER 5:7 NIV**

A re you carrying an extra set of worries with you today? Peter encouraged believers to cast all their anxiety on the Lord. Notice the word *all*. God is asking you to take the entire sum of your anxieties—past concerns, present worries, and future burdens—and roll them onto Him. He doesn't want you to carry a single one. Oh, what a day when your burdens roll off your heart and firmly onto the Lord!

What can you know about the One who has taken all your worries? He cares for you. You are His concern, and your worries are vastly important to Him. Your worries may crush you, but they are like a feather to the Creator of the universe. So let the One who cares for you carry you and all your worries today.

*Lord, today I cast all my cares on You. Thank You for Your care and concern for me. Amen.*

# Instruments of His Love

Love one another, just as I have loved you.

**JOHN 15:12**

I f you are ever tempted to wonder about God's ways, discover a new encouragement knowing His love is working in and through you. You are an instrument of His love, expressing His mercy and compassion to hungry, hurting hearts. People need God's love.

So many in the world only know a fleeting kind of commitment. You can give God's unconditional love freely and extravagantly when you rely on God's indwelling Holy Spirit to empower you. The Holy Spirit pours out God's love in your heart (Romans 5:5), transforms you (2 Corinthians 3:18), and empowers you to tell the world about Christ (Acts 1:8). Always remember, you may be the only visible demonstration of God's love for someone in your life today. Take time to give His love away to everyone you meet in the course of your everyday life.

*Lord, will You love others in and through me? Remind me of Your love with each person I meet today. Amen.*

# Extravagant Grace

Those who receive the abundance of grace
and of the gift of righteousness will reign
in life through the One, Jesus Christ.

**ROMANS 5:17**

I f you ask a child why she loves Christmas so much, she is likely to squeal, "The presents!" Most people are like children when it comes to gifts. They can't wait to see what's inside.

God gives the best gifts. All His gifts are given to you by His grace.

God gives extravagantly because His grace is extravagant. You might think of grace as God's Riches At Christ's Expense. It's costly, and it's made possible only by Christ's death on the cross, but it's freely poured out on you without measure. Grace is a gift—the free, unmerited favor of God. You can't earn it. You don't deserve it. But you must receive it.

Today, will you receive the extravagant gift of God's grace? If so, then begin pulling off the ribbon. Open God's Word and discover all the magnificent gifts of God's grace bestowed freely on you.

*Lord, thank You for giving me Your*
*extravagant grace. Amen.*

# The Gift of God's Grace

Jesus Christ our Lord, through whom
we have received grace…

**ROMANS 1:4-5**

God's grace gift is at the heart of all God does toward you, for you, and in you. Grace finds you, saves you, and keeps you. Grace opens the floodgates so He can pour His endless love into your life, moment by moment, on into eternity. When you understand the nature of God's gracious gift in your own life, it seems almost too good to be true. How can God give abounding gifts to us even though we don't earn or deserve them? We find the answer when we look at the cross and realize the cost. Christ's incarnation—His life on earth, death on the cross, resurrection after three days, and ascension into heaven—opens your eyes to the precious possibilities for grace in you. If Jesus gave His life that you might know His extravagant grace, then grace is infinitely valuable and all-powerful. Receive His grace today and unwrap the gift.

*Lord, thank You for pouring out Your grace on
me freely and extravagantly today. Amen.*

# How Then Shall We Be Saved?

For by grace you have been saved through faith;
and that not of yourselves, it is the gift of God; not
as a result of works, so that no one may boast.

**EPHESIANS 2:8-9**

If people are good, are they exempt from paying the penalty of their sins? If people have all the money in the world, can they buy an entry pass into heaven? The answers to those questions are found in the Bible. God says you can't earn your way into His presence. You cannot buy a ticket to heaven or pay for forgiveness of sins. How then can anyone be saved?

The answer is wrapped up in God's magnificent grace. According to Paul in Ephesians 2:8, you are saved by grace through faith. Will you enjoy the free gift of God's grace? If you have never stepped into the garden of grace, will you receive Christ into your life?

*Lord, today I say yes to Your grace. Help me never try to earn what I've been freely given. Amen.*

# Is His Grace Really Enough?

Where sin increased, grace abounded all the more.

**ROMANS 5:20**

---

"But my sin is just too great," some have said. "God could not possibly forgive me." Maybe similar thoughts have crossed your own mind. Perhaps even now the doubts continue to linger: *What if I'm really not forgiven?* Settle forever your relationship with your Lord. If you have received Christ and experienced new life in Him through the work of the Holy Spirit, you can know your sins are forgiven. God forgave all your sins—past, present, and future—through Christ's death on the cross.

Maybe you're thinking, *I see how my past and present sins are forgiven. But what about future sins?* Your past and present sins were actually future sins 2000 years ago, when Christ gave His life on the cross for you. When you doubt your forgiveness and the power of God's grace, just look at the cross. Christ's death on the cross was enough. He promises (Acts 10:43).

*Lord, thank You for assuring me of the*
*powerful truth that I'm forgiven! Amen.*

# Three Crosses, Two Sinners, and a King

Two others also, who were criminals,
were being led away to be put to death with Him.
When they came to the place called The Skull,
there they crucified Him and the criminals.

**LUKE 23:32-33**

-----------------------------------

Three crosses stood on Calvary with three men nearing death. One was the King of kings, and the other two were criminals. The King was bearing our griefs, carrying our sorrows, and being crushed for our iniquities (Isaiah 53:4-5). But the criminals, one hanging on His right and the other on His left, were dying in their sins. For a brief moment, time brushed up against eternity. One criminal mocked Jesus, betraying an unrepentant heart. The other pleaded with Jesus to remember him in His kingdom, displaying great faith.

The cross always stands between two choices: fear or faith, rebellion or repentance. What is your choice today as you look at Jesus? Will you say yes and run to Him in faith?

*Lord, I come to You in faith today believing*
*You are my King and my Lord. Amen.*

# Forgiven on the Cross

Truly I say to you, today you shall
be with Me in Paradise.

**LUKE 23:43**

---

Seeing Jesus on the cross gives you a glimpse of His heart for you. Jesus, the sinless King, was led like a lamb to slaughter. While dying a criminal's death on a cross, He turned to face one of His own. In the depth of His passion, Jesus took time to forgive and assure a repentant sinner. "Truly I say to you, today you shall be with Me in Paradise." The word *truly* must have been one of the greatest words a dying man could hear. With that word, Jesus assured him that he could be absolutely certain of what Jesus was saying. The doomed criminal was promised an eternal destiny with Jesus in Paradise. If Jesus gave such happy words to a dying man in the depth of His own pain, just imagine His encouragement and love for you today.

*Lord, thank You for Your great love for*
*sinners—even one like me. Amen.*

# Growing Deep in God's Grace

Grow in the grace and knowledge of
our Lord and Savior Jesus Christ.

**2 PETER 3:18**

Thriving gardens with bountiful, blooming flowers require fertile soil. Our spirits also need constant nourishment, and God has placed you in the perfect environment where you can grow spiritually healthy and mature. You blossom in the atmosphere of His extravagant grace. First you are saved by grace. And now you can thrive and grow in His magnificent grace.

Are you trying to gain His love and acceptance? Are you working hard for His smile and His favor? You already have what you desire. God is the God of all grace (1 Peter 5:10), He sits on a throne of grace (Hebrews 4:16), and He showers you with the riches of His grace (Ephesians 1:7-8).

Most people try to make you pay for your shortcomings. But Jesus, full of grace and truth, has already paid for everything on your behalf. His grace has already given you everything you need.

*Lord, thank You for the vast ocean*
*of Your abundant grace. I rest in Your*
*loving, comforting arms today. Amen.*

# The Garden of Grace

We have peace with God through our
Lord Jesus Christ, through whom also we
have obtained our introduction by faith
into this grace in which we stand.

**ROMANS 5:1-2**

---

Grace is like a garden that you are privileged to live in every day. It's a place of delights and brings richness and joy and peace in your life. If you have ever walked through a beautiful garden, you know the peace and the rest that washes over you. In the garden of grace, you can stop, relax, and converse with your Lord. This communion is intimate, private, and personal. No one can touch this secret garden of God's grace.

All who have ever walked with God have known and experienced the garden. Many great lovers of God have enjoyed the gifts found in the garden. God has planted you in grace. Today, will you find a comfortable bench in God's garden and sit awhile with Him?

*Lord, I love Your garden of grace and look
forward to more time with You, where I will learn
about You and all You've given me. Amen.*

# The Riches of His Grace

In Him we have redemption through His
blood, the forgiveness of our trespasses,
according to the riches of His grace.

**EPHESIANS 1:7**

A young man convicted of a capital offense stood
before his judge for sentencing. The judge read
the man's offenses and levied the death penalty. The
convicted criminal hung his head in shame and despair.
But then a shocking turn of events occurred. The judge
stood, removed his robes, stepped down, and walked
around to face the prisoner. He turned to the bailiff,
held out his hands and said, "I will take this young
man's place and pay the price for his crime. Young man,
you are free to go."

Of course, in real life, this could never happen. But
for you, just such an amazing exchange has occurred.
God gave His only begotten Son so you might be set
free and receive the wealth of His grace. Today, thank
the Lord for the riches of His grace.

*Lord, thank You for bestowing on me, an undeserving
sinner, the riches of Your grace. Amen.*

# The Great Rescue

He rescued us from the domain of darkness, and
transferred us to the kingdom of His beloved Son.

**COLOSSIANS 1:13**

---

In the fairy tale *Snow White and the Seven Dwarfs*, a
princess falls into a deep sleep. She is saved when a
handsome prince, while riding his horse through the
woods, finds her and kisses her, thus breaking the spell
that had imprisoned her in darkness. They ride off to
his castle and live happily ever after.

Jesus has accomplished a much greater rescue than
the kind described in the fairy tale. You are no longer
held captive in the slave market of sin. He has paid the
price for you, buying your freedom. Jesus has brought
you to His castle, so to speak, for He has transferred
you to His kingdom. You no longer live in the darkness of sin and death. Instead, you live in the garden of
grace, where Christ rules.

*Lord, thank You for rescuing me and placing me in*
*the garden of grace, where I live with You. Amen.*

# Have You Learned to Fly?

Therefore, if anyone is in Christ, he is
a new creature; the old things passed
away; behold, new things have come.

**2 CORINTHIANS 5:17**

Through a metamorphosis, a caterpillar forms a soft shell, called a cocoon. In the cocoon, the caterpillar is gradually transformed into something new—a butterfly with wings and the ability to fly.

The newness of life you experience in Christ is more like a metamorphosis than a simple alteration of the same old thing. You become a brand-new creation when you are born again in Christ. You are indwelt by the Holy Spirit, transformed within, and given a new life with God. You're not what you were. Jesus transforms you and is in the process of making you the woman He wants you to be. Get ready for new things in your life, for Jesus has made you brand-new.

*Lord, thank You for making me the woman*
*You want me to be, transforming me*
*within, and giving me a new life. Amen.*

# Have You Looked in
# the Mirror Lately?

*By the grace of God I am what I am.*

**1 CORINTHIANS 15:10**

---

Have you ever watched a young child walk by a tall mirror? Immediately she stops and gazes at her image in wonder. A mirror never seems to lose its fascination, even when wrinkles begin lining the face with age.

God has given you the mirror of His Word. When you look in it, you discover who you really are by His grace. You are a child of God, adopted into the family of God. You are like a butterfly, designed to soar with God in His magnificent kingdom. Every day, when you choose to look in the mirror of God's Word, you will discover your true beauty in Christ. And friend, you *are* beautiful! Jesus is altogether lovely and gives you His beauty, shining from within you. So today, look in the mirror and discover how beautiful you really are.

*Lord, thank You for making me*
*beautiful. Shine in me today. Amen.*

# All God's Gifts

Every good thing given and every perfect gift is
from above, coming down from the Father of lights,
with whom there is no variation or shifting shadow.

**JAMES 1:17**

When everything around you is falling apart, you still have the assuring presence of your unchanging heavenly Father. He never changes, so His grace continues to give and give and give some more. Grace, by its very nature, pours out unmerited gifts on undeserving sinners. So even if you are in the lowest place imaginable, you can know you will still receive good and perfect gifts of grace from your Father.

Do you need a gift from God today? Perhaps you are experiencing very little kindness or compassion from other people right now. Friend, even in your adversity, you have God's love, which is greater than anything an earthly relationship can offer. Run to Him today in the garden of grace where you live and experience a new touch of His love.

*Lord, I need the touch of Your love today,*
*flowing from Your gracious heart. Amen.*

# Who Is Your God?

After you have suffered for a little
while, the God of all grace...

**1 PETER 5:10**

God wants you to understand a powerful truth in difficult days when the fog of pain obscures reality. When you suffer, God wants you to know that He is the God of *all* grace. That little word *all* includes everything you need. God is saying that He has more than enough grace to match your need, desperate as your trouble is. He sees the depth of your trouble, for He has taken the time to tell you the measure of His grace.

You may be thinking, *My trouble is too great.* He knows your thoughts, and He is clarifying the matter for you. He is the God of *all* grace, enough for all trouble, even your trouble. God sees, He cares, and He encourages you in your trials. Regardless of how great your difficulty may be, God is greater. He is always enough. Draw near to your God today and drink in the comfort of His infinite grace.

*Lord, thank You for assuring me of Your grace,*
*enough for the most desperate times. Amen.*

# Grace for Suffering

The God of all grace, who called you to His
eternal glory in Christ, will Himself perfect,
confirm, strengthen and establish you.

**1 PETER 5:10**

---

What gifts of grace can you anticipate when you are suffering? You are actually promised special gifts, custom-designed for road-weary grace walkers. First, God gives you the promise of a happy ending to your story despite the rocks in your path. He has given you eternal glory in Christ. No one can touch your future with Jesus in heaven. And second, He has given you His guarantee that the floodwaters of your life will eventually recede. The suffering lasts only "a little while." Take a deep breath and exhale with a huge sigh of relief. The trial you thought would last forever will eventually end in God's perfect timetable.

God is going to use your experience for His glory and make you beautiful and strong. Did you have any idea of the beauty of God's grace for you in the hard times? Thank your Lord and prepare to unwrap these special gifts.

*Lord, thank You for Your custom-
designed gifts for me today. Amen.*

# Overflowing Grace

God is able to make all grace abound to you, so
that always having all sufficiency in everything, you
may have an abundance for every good deed.

**2 CORINTHIANS 9:8**

---

Grace in God's garden is necessary for every area of your life, especially when you are given seemingly impossible tasks and responsibilities. God never expected you to go it alone out in the cold, handling life yourself. Perhaps you have felt discouraged and completely inadequate. God promises "all sufficiency in everything." You will have enough. In fact, you will have so much that you will be satisfied and content.

Think about how confidently you can spend money when you know you have more than enough in your bank account. Overflowing grace gives you that same feeling of confident assurance.

When you walk into an overwhelming situation, stop for a moment and remember God's abundant grace, promising everything you need. Then rest in assurance of God's adequate provision.

*Lord, thank You for promising me an*
*abundance of grace so I can do everything*
*You ask me to do today. Amen.*

# The Power of Weakness

He has said to me, "My grace is sufficient for you,
for power is perfected in weakness." Most gladly,
therefore, I will rather boast about my weaknesses...
for when I am weak, then I am strong.

**2 CORINTHIANS 12:9-10**

We have a misconception that the longer we walk with Jesus, the stronger we automatically become. Actually, the opposite can happen. Thankfully, Paul, one of the greatest Christians of all time, is our teacher. He appeared to be strong, but in fact, he was actually weak. He didn't have just one weakness, but many. Paul's weaknesses qualified him for God's strength.

If you feel weak, you can find encouragement and rejoice. God's grace gives you Christ's power, making you strong enough for every task. What responsibilities are on your task list today? Choose any of the most difficult assignments and hear God whisper these words to you: *My grace is sufficient for you.* Then launch out in confidence, drawing on the strength and power of Christ.

*Lord, thank You that when I am*
*weak, I am strong. Amen.*

# How Shall We Live?

What then? Shall we sin because we are not
under law but under grace? May it never be!

**ROMANS 6:15**

Our freedom in grace doesn't give us a license to sin. Some have thought, *It doesn't matter what I do because I'm not under law, but under grace.* Paul would respond now as he did then: "May it never be!" Living in the garden of grace gives you the freedom to say yes to God and no to sin. Life under grace affords you the privilege of following God's leading in life. God's grace never leads to rebellion. Instead, His grace gives you the Holy Spirit's power within to say yes to Him. And when you yield to Him, you will enjoy the blessings of obedience.

Obedience to God is your way of life in the garden of grace. Each obedient step carries you along the path of God's purpose and plan for you. Today, will you say yes to God and no to sin, and enjoy the blessed benefits of God's grace?

*Lord, help me say yes to You as I live
in the garden of grace. Amen.*

# When You Sin

If we confess our sins, He is faithful and
righteous to forgive us our sins and to
cleanse us from all unrighteousness.

**1 JOHN 1:9**

---

You resolve to live by grace through faith, and you begin to enjoy the garden of God's grace and the blessings of obedience. But then you sin. Is your life with the Lord now hopeless? Are there no second chances? Should you give up?

John shows you God's perspective now that you are His child living in the garden of grace. He invites you to confess your sins. Confession means you agree with God that you have sinned. When you run to God in confession, you receive forgiveness and cleansing.

Have you ever gotten covered with dust and dirt from head to toe? You stepped into the shower and felt the refreshing water wash away every bit of dirt. Confession and forgiveness produce that clean feeling and make your life seem brand-new again. Today, if you have sinned, don't wait any longer. Confess and be blessed.

*Lord, thank You for your forgiveness*
*in my life every day. Amen.*

# The Gift of Your Future

Now may our Lord Jesus Christ Himself
and God our Father, who has loved us and
given us eternal comfort and good hope
by grace, comfort and strengthen your
hearts in every good work and word.

**2 THESSALONIANS 2:16-17**

———————————————

Grace gives you hope for an amazing future. You are given the promise of everlasting life. Paul calls your grace gift an "eternal comfort and good hope." Regardless of what happens today, you have a future that never changes, can never be withdrawn, and lasts forever. You always know the rest of your story while you live in the present. You can smile at the future, for you have the hope of heaven filled with never-ending consolation, encouragement, and solace from God. Grace gives you a "good hope." When you hope, you are Holding On with Patient Expectation for God's fulfillment of His promise. And you can be confident that God always keeps His promises.

*Lord, thank You for giving me eternal comfort and*
*hope and enabling me to smile at the future. Amen.*

HOPE

# The God of Hope

Now may the God of hope fill you with
all joy and peace in believing.

**ROMANS 15:13**

Have you ever felt as though you lost your hope? If you know the Lord, you can never lose your hope, for you can never lose God, who is a God of hope. He is the source and the object of your hope. When you enter into a relationship with God through Christ, you enjoy a forever relationship with Him. Because He is with you forever, His hope is always available for you. When you run to Him, He pours hope into your aching heart. The more you know God, the more you will hope.

When you learn a new truth about God in your quiet time, you find a powerful promise leading you to a greater hope. Today, if your heart feels low on hope, open your Bible, read a psalm, and write out everything you learn about God. You will discover new hope for your soul.

*Lord, thank You for giving me hope today*
*because of who You are. Amen.*

# Finding Hope

You will abound in hope by the
power of the Holy Spirit.

**ROMANS 15:13**

------------------------------------

Have you ever felt so discouraged you wished someone could flip a switch that would change your attitude? Your attitude can change over time because you have a permanent, unlimited, inner source of hope. An overflowing well of hope constantly flows from within because you are indwelt by the Holy Spirit. His power brings new hope into your life just when you need it. When you run to the Lord, He causes your hope to abound, overflow, and increase through the Holy Spirit.

You will notice times when your hope seems to ebb. Life's circumstances challenge your hope. In the fight of faith, sometimes your emotions give way to despair. But the indwelling Holy Spirit can give you supernatural power to hope even when you seem to have no hope. Never give up. Always run to God and drink from His overflowing river of hope.

*Lord, thank You for Your promise of abounding*
*hope through the power of the Holy Spirit. Amen.*

# How Can I Have Hope?

This I recall to my mind,
Therefore I have hope.
The LORD's lovingkindnesses indeed never cease,
For His compassions never fail.
They are new every morning;
Great is Your faithfulness.

**LAMENTATIONS 3:21-23**

The whole world would love to know the secret to hope. Empty, aimless people spend millions of dollars trying to build lives that are free from despair. Jeremiah discovered God's secret in the crucible of his own despair and despondency. In the midst of his lament, he stopped and turned his mind in a new direction. Look closely at Jeremiah's focus, and you'll notice he found some of God's greatest promises in His character and His works.

God's promises are the secret to hope in your life. The Bible, God's love letter written just for you, is filled with thousands of promises, all custom designed to fuel your life with constant hope. Today, if you would like a dose of hope, open God's Word and latch on to one of His promises.

*Lord, thank You for Your promises, which You have designed to keep my heart filled with hope. Amen.*

# God Is at Work

God is working in you, giving you the desire
and the power to do what pleases him.

**PHILIPPIANS 2:13 NLT**

Do you sometimes lose your focus in life? Do you ever wonder about your life's purpose? When you find yourself in times like these, let the promise of God guide your thinking. Maybe you have just experienced a shocking turn of events. What is God doing? You can know that He is at work in you. He is accomplishing His purpose and carrying out His will.

Corrie ten Boom surely must have found great comfort and hope in this promise when she and her sister were imprisoned at Ravensbruck concentration camp. Even there in that dark place, God was still at work in Corrie and Betsie and the hundreds who heard the gospel and were saved. You too can know that God is at work, even if you don't immediately see His results. You may not completely understand until you see Him face-to-face. But you can hope in His work now because of His great promise.

*Lord, thank You for working out*
*Your will in me. Amen.*

# God Will Help You

Do not fear, for I am with you;
Do not anxiously look about you, for I am your God.
I will strengthen you, surely I will help you,
Surely I will uphold you with My
righteous right hand.

**ISAIAH 41:10**

-------------------------------

When you are faced with a fear that is overtaking your heart and soul, you can find hope in God's promise to help you. He says we need not fear or "anxiously look about." God does not want you to allow fear or anxiety to paralyze you. He promises you His presence, strength, and help for your fearful and anxious moments.

When you read this promise, notice the repetition of *surely*, offering you God's own personal guarantee of help for you in your trial. No fear is so great that God's help and presence is not greater still. Live in the light of God's promise and enjoy confident assurance instead of worry and fear.

*Lord, thank You for helping me when*
*I'm anxious and afraid. Amen.*

# I Can't, but He Can

I can do all things through Him who strengthens me.

**PHILIPPIANS 4:13**

-----------------------------

God is going to ask you to accomplish tasks that are beyond your strength or ability. You can count on His high calling in your life. But rest assured, He never intended for you to do His work in your own strength. He intends to accomplish great and mighty things in and through you. When you receive His assignment and cry out to Him, *I can't do it*, learn to add the words *but You can!*

Paul learned this secret when he said, "I can do all things through Him who strengthens me." He spoke with assurance, not arrogance. He was counting on God's promise of strength. Just imagine how easily God can accomplish your task. After all, as Creator of the universe, He can create something out of nothing. You can count on Him for enough strength to match your need today.

*Lord, as I think about all You have asked of me,*
*I can only say, "I can't, but You can!" Amen.*

# God's Smile Is Better

For God is not unjust so as to forget your
work and the love which you have shown
toward His name, in having ministered
and in still ministering to the saints.

**HEBREWS 6:10**

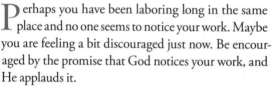

Perhaps you have been laboring long in the same place and no one seems to notice your work. Maybe you are feeling a bit discouraged just now. Be encouraged by the promise that God notices your work, and He applauds it.

God's smile is worth so much more than man's applause. He notices the small touches you give, even if no one else notices your actions. God saw the day you handpicked a present for a friend. He was there when you cared for a sick loved one. He noticed when you lovingly cooked a meal and cleaned your house. All you do is a ministry in the name of the Lord. God notices, and He is smiling.

*Lord, thank You for the assurance that You*
*notice the love I've shown toward You*
*in ministering to others. Amen.*

# You Are Never Alone

He Himself has said, "I will never desert you, nor
will I ever forsake you," so that we confidently
say, "The Lord is my helper, I will not be afraid."

**HEBREWS 13:5-6**

---

Have you ever been disappointed by someone? You
thought that person would be there for you, but
in the end, you were left alone. Parents may disappoint
families and spouses may leave, but God *never* deserts
His children. He promises, "I will never desert you, nor
will I ever forsake you."

Maybe you needed to hear those words because you
have felt as though you were on your own with no one
to help you. The Lord is your helper, and He is Maker
of heaven and earth. What an encouragement to know
that the Creator of the universe is your helper! What a
blessing to know the presence of the One who can create
something out of nothing! You are never alone. God
is with you, and He is faithful.

*Lord, thank You for assuring me today that You
will never desert me or forsake me. Amen.*

# All Good Things

They who seek the LORD shall not
be in want of any good thing.

**PSALM 34:10**

---

God promises that when you seek Him, you will never lack for any good thing. If it's good, you'll have it. If it's not good, you really don't want it anyway. The promise of all good things from God gives you abundant security. You can know without a doubt that God is liberal in His giving. He is not reluctant to pour out His blessings. He is graciously generous and even gives His best to us undeserving sinners.

If you don't have something you desperately want, then take comfort in this promise. Either God has something better for you or He is waiting for His perfect timing. Timing is everything in the physical realm and in the spiritual realm. You can trust that God's gifts and His timing are perfect. And you can trust His promise today.

*Lord, today I trust You to give me all good
things in Your time and in Your way. Amen.*

# Be Not Afraid

He answered me,
And delivered me from all my fears.

**PSALM 34:4**

---

Are you afraid of something or someone today? Or are you anxious about a multitude of situations in your life? Perhaps you are so afraid that your fears have stacked up and are threatening to bury you. God can give you hope when you are afraid. When you seek Him, He will answer you and deliver you from all your fears. With God, you can run valiantly toward any fear, just as David ran toward Goliath.

Avoidance actually feeds fear. Deal with your fear by taking it to God and trusting Him to deliver you. Fretting about your fear and running from it are actually more crippling than the fear itself. When you rely on God's strength to deliver you and step out in faith, fear begins to dissipate. So today, dear friend, don't be afraid. Instead, run to God and ask Him to deliver you from your fears. He promises He will.

*Lord, thank You for delivering me from*
*every one of my fears. Amen.*

# God Will Supply Your Needs

My God will supply all your needs according
to His riches in glory in Christ Jesus.

**PHILIPPIANS 4:19**

God's promise of provision gives you hope when you are in need. God is your provider and will give you what you need when you need it. His promise to "supply" your needs means He will give to you abundantly and liberally. You may be thinking, *Yes, but He hasn't given me what I want.* Maybe you have not yet considered something on God's mind. Perhaps His plan includes a new direction. Sometimes God will say no to something good in order to give you the very best. He is giving out of His riches, so He never lacks supply and will generously pour out His blessings on you.

Take all your needs to Him today and watch to see what He will do. He will supply your needs. He promises.

*Lord, thank You for promising to supply
all my needs. I look to You for every good
thing in Your perfect timing. Amen.*

# God Speaks with Purpose

It is the same with my word.
I send it out, and it always produces fruit.
It will accomplish all I want it to,
And it will prosper everywhere I send it.

**ISAIAH 55:11 NLT**

---

When you open the pages of God's Word and start reading, remember that you are not alone. God is with you, and He has something to say to you. With every word He speaks, He promises that your life has meaning and purpose. So you can confidently read, knowing He is going to speak to you. His indwelling Spirit will cause His Word to come alive.

When you read, something may stand out—a verse, a phrase, or sometimes even just a word. When something in the Bible seems significant, stop and pay attention to what He is saying. You may discover something you had never seen before, something that can transform your heart and alter the course of your life.

*Lord, thank You for promising to speak*
*through Your Word and to use it to accomplish*
*Your purpose in my life. Amen.*

# God's Ways

My ways are far beyond anything you could imagine.
For just as the heavens are higher than the earth,
so my ways are higher than your ways
and my thoughts higher than your thoughts.

**ISAIAH 55:8-9 NLT**

---

Have you sometimes wondered about God's ways? Maybe you've thought, *What in the world is God doing?* God's ways are beyond your own thought processes. He is never limited to our human options. God can accomplish the impossible. He is never without resource or strength. And He can create something out of nothing.

Perhaps your current circumstances are so confusing that you're ready to throw your hands in the air and give up. Dear friend, even if you can't seem to understand the circumstances, you *can* know the God who holds your life in His capable hands. And the more you know Him, the more you will trust Him.

*Lord, today I admit I don't understand Your ways, but I thank You that I can know You and trust You. Amen.*

# A Bright and Glorious Hope

The sufferings of this present time are
not worthy to be compared with the
glory that is to be revealed to us.

**ROMANS 8:18**

---

A woman diagnosed with a terminal disease presented her pastor with an unusual request: "I want to be buried with a fork in my right hand." She told him that her favorite part of any meal was the moment when someone said, "Keep your fork." Those words assured her of a wonderful dessert. She said, "I want people to wonder about that fork in my hand. Tell them, 'The best is yet to come.'"

Our eternal future brings hope in our present sufferings. At the age of 17, Joni Eareckson Tada became a quadriplegic after a diving accident. She often shares that the sufferings and sorrow that currently assail us aren't worthy to be compared with that which waits over the horizon. You can be assured today of the bright and glorious hope of eternity, even in your darkest trials.

*Lord, sometimes today's darkness obscures the light of eternity with You in my eternal home. Help me find hope in remembering that the best is yet to come. Amen.*

# Out of This World

They were looking for a better place, a heavenly
homeland. That is why God is not ashamed to be
called their God, for he has prepared a city for them.

**HEBREWS 11:16 NLT**

When someone asks you how you are, what is your response? One man has a unique reply: "I'm one step closer to heaven." Aren't those words magnificently true! If you are a child of God, your home is not on earth but with Christ in heaven.

Are you discouraged today? Had you thought that perhaps nothing could part the dark clouds and brighten your life? You have a hope that is literally out of this world! Look up and take heart in the truth that one day you will step from time into eternity. Then you can breathe the deepest sigh of relief and say with true joy, "I'm home."

> *Lord, help me stop looking down and start looking*
> *up at You and my hope of heaven, where I will*
> *one day truly smile and say, "I'm home." Amen.*

# A Future and a Hope

"For I know the plans that I have for you,"
declares the LORD, "plans for welfare and not
for calamity to give you a future and a hope."

**JEREMIAH 29:11**

---

Have you ever wondered about your future? Maybe you have felt discouraged, thinking your circumstances are beyond hope. God promises that He has a plan for your life and that you have a future and a hope. You may not know what your future holds, but you can know the God who holds your future. He is trustworthy and faithful.

The more you know your Lord, the more your confidence will grow. Turn to the promises in the psalms and discover God is your refuge (Psalm 46:1) your light, and your salvation (Psalm 27:1). His love and faithfulness reach to the heavens (Psalm 36:5). Rest in these promises with a steadfast confidence in God's promise to carry out His plan for your life.

*Lord, I trust You with today and with all my*
*tomorrows until one day I see You face-to-face. Amen.*

# In the Waiting Room

And the Scriptures give us hope and
encouragement as we wait patiently
for God's promises to be fulfilled.

**ROMANS 15:4 NLT**

G od is more than a match for any desperate hour.
His promises are tethers to hold you close to Him.
Hope grasps each promise in the waiting room of life,
enabling you to Hold On with Patient Expectation.
Other men see only a hopeless end, but the Christian
rejoices in an endless hope.

How can you have an endless hope? Open your
Bible and grasp one of God's promises. When you carry
God's amazing promises as great treasure, your gaze
moves from the secular to the spiritual and from the
temporal to the eternal. And then you will enjoy a hope-
filled life.

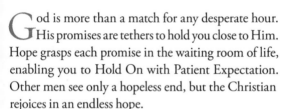

*Lord, today I feel as though I am in life's waiting
room with no end in sight. Help me to rest my
eyes on Your promises, filling my gaze only with
truth from Your Word. Then I will rejoice
in the endless hope I have in You. Amen.*

# Heaven Is Your Hope

He will wipe every tear from their eyes; and
there will no longer be any death; there will
no longer be any mourning, or crying, or
pain; the first things have passed away.

**REVELATION 21:4**

---

The promise of heaven brings the greatest hope of all God's promises, especially for those who suffer daily with pain. Did you know that God stores all your tears in a bottle (Psalm 56:8)? When you imagine God collecting your tears, you realize how very precious you are to Him.

Heaven will bring you into a completely new existence. One day God is going to personally wipe every tear from your eyes. You will never again mourn, cry, or experience pain. There is no sickness in heaven. There are no disabilities in heaven. You won't see any wheelchairs, walkers, or canes. Doesn't that make you smile today? Having so much to look forward to in heaven gives you a great reason to hope. Find comfort and encouragement in heaven's promise today.

*Lord, thank You for the ultimate*
*promise of heaven. Amen.*

# TRUST

# The Key That Unlocks the Door

Those who know Your name will
put their trust in You.

**PSALM 9:10**

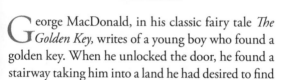

George MacDonald, in his classic fairy tale *The Golden Key,* writes of a young boy who found a golden key. When he unlocked the door, he found a stairway taking him into a land he had desired to find and longed to know from his earliest years.

Imagine living in a beautiful land where you could trust God with the details of your life and experience the great adventure of knowing Him as a result. Is this just a fairy-tale? No! Is this life possible today? Yes! The key that unlocks the door to a life of trust in God is a knowledge of God's names. David discovered this secret when he said, "Those who know Your name will put their trust in You." David's discovery opens the way to a whole new type of living. Knowing God's names means you know and trust Him.

*O Lord, help me open the pages of my Bible today and use the key of Your names to unlock the door to a life of trusting in You. Amen.*

# Facing the Giants

Some boast in chariots and some in horses,
But we will boast in the names of the Lord, our God.

**PSALM 20:7**

---

Life's troubles often seem greater than your dwindling trust in God. You can develop giant-sized trust in God only by facing giant impossibilities. If you face immense difficulty, you can know that God is taking you to a new place in your adventure with Him. In this seemingly strange new experience, you will gain a greater view of God, and you will receive what you need to trust God to overcome your difficulty, whatever it may be.

David exercised a new and greater trust in God the day he met the giant Goliath. Because David's view was enhanced by understanding God's greatness, he saw Goliath as a midget in comparison. When your eyes turn to God, your trials seem less devastating and ominous. Looking to God, you will trust God more in the midst of your giant trouble.

*Lord, I'm facing a giant today and need
a greater view of You. Give me eyes to see
You and a heart to trust You. Amen.*

# No Worries

Do not be worried about your life.

**MATTHEW 6:25**

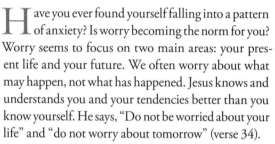

Have you ever found yourself falling into a pattern of anxiety? Is worry becoming the norm for you? Worry seems to focus on two main areas: your present life and your future. We often worry about what may happen, not what has happened. Jesus knows and understands you and your tendencies better than you know yourself. He says, "Do not be worried about your life" and "do not worry about tomorrow" (verse 34).

A.J. Russell asks, what would we think about a man who walks through a field and frets "because ahead there lay a river he might not be able to cross, when all the time that river was spanned by a bridge? And what if he had a friend who knew the way?"

You can trust your Lord today to anticipate your needs and guide you through your difficult days. And remember, people who follow Jesus always get to their destination.

*Lord, today I give all my worries to You and trust You to lead and guide me into Your plan for me. Amen.*

# The Flier and the Catcher

Our soul waits for the LORD;
He is our help and our shield.
For our heart rejoices in Him,
Because we trust in His holy name.

**PSALM 33:20-21**

-----

Trapeze artists fly through the air and perform death-defying feats. Many of those who watch may not realize the unique relationship between the flier and the catcher. The flier swings high above the crowd, releases the trapeze, and arcs into the air. For a moment, which may seem like an eternity, the flier is suspended in air. His job is to be as still and motionless as he can. The flier must never try to catch the catcher. Instead of anxiously flailing his arms, he waits in absolute trust. The skilled flier trusts the catcher to be at the right spot, reach out, and grab hold.

In the great adventure of knowing God, accomplishing the sometimes scary twists and turns in your life requires that you let go of some things, feel yourself suspended and waiting, and be still and wait as you trust Him to catch you.

*Lord, I feel like a flier in midair, so I will
trust in You, my Catcher. I will wait for
You and Your perfect timing. Amen.*

# Trust in the Lord

Trust in the LORD with all your heart.

**PROVERBS 3:5**

---

Author Brennan Manning recounts a conversation in which his spiritual director told him, "Brennan, you don't need any more insights into the faith. You've got enough insights to last you 300 years. The most urgent need in your life is to trust what you've received." Can you relate to that?

Maybe you feel as though you know a lot of truths from the Bible. But do you really trust God's Word in your everyday life? God desires your deepest trust. In fact, the people of Israel were exiled to Babylon partly because they chose to depend on man instead of trust God. God wants you to trust in Him with all your heart. What does it mean to trust? You can think of trust as Total Reliance Under Stress and Trial. Today, take God's Word and totally rely on what He says when you experience stress and trial.

*Lord, help me to trust You today*
*with all my heart. Amen.*

# Do You Trust the Lord?

But as for me, I trust in You, O LORD.

**PSALM 31:14**

---

A tightrope walker stood on a tightrope high above a crowd of onlookers. He cried out, "How many of you believe I can walk across this tightrope?"

They all cried out, "You can do it!"

"How many of you believe I can walk across the tightrope with this wheelbarrow?"

"You can do it!" they yelled again.

Then he asked, "Who will be the first one to get in the wheelbarrow?" Silence. The crowd had said they believed, but none of them actually trusted.

Maybe you feel as though God is asking you to get in the wheelbarrow. Your situation may appear impossible. Choose to trust and watch God take you through the trial. Echo the psalmist's words: "But as for me, I trust in You, O LORD."

*Lord, today I choose to trust in You. Amen.*

# Knowing God's Names

Every day I will bless You,
And I will praise Your name forever and ever.

**PSALM 145:2**

G od gives you His names in His Word with a great purpose. He wants you to know and trust Him. His names reveal His character. The more you know who God is, the more you will love and trust Him. From Genesis to Revelation, God reveals countless truths about Himself.

Think about His revelation for a moment. Why would He give you so many truths about who He is, what He does, and what He says? He does this for one primary reason—He wants you to know and experience Him in a vibrant, intimate, ongoing relationship. When you read God's Word, you realize God wears His heart on His sleeve, constantly showing you His thoughts and feelings. The world believes God is distant and impersonal, but we know He is near and intimate with us. Take time today to know and love your God more.

*Lord, thank You for revealing so much of Yourself*
*to me. I delight to know You more. Amen.*

# Depending on God

The LORD is my Shepherd,
I shall not want.

**PSALM 23:1**

---

The names of God reveal truth about God and also truth about you. Knowing the Lord as your Shepherd reveals your need for a shepherd's care and comfort. Perhaps you enjoy an independent lifestyle and run from dependence on anything or anyone. The Lord wants you to stop depending on yourself and start depending on Him.

When you learn that God is *El Shaddai*, you realize His all-sufficiency in your life. You also learn that you need Him in every circumstance. You are never enough for a situation—even when you think you are. Once you realize how much you need your Lord, you will learn to trust in Him.

How do you need the Lord today? Will you draw near to Him for His comfort and care?

*Lord, today I thank You that You are*
*everything I need in my life. Amen.*

# Not Your Life

I have been crucified with Christ; and it is no longer I who live, but Christ lives in me.

**GALATIANS 2:20**

A young woman called her father, a pastor, and said, "Dad, I just don't know what to do with my life."

Her father replied, "Well, that's your problem. It's not your life. It's His life. I was there the day you gave your life to Christ. Now you belong to Him."

Paul assures us of a supernatural existence in which we no longer live, but Christ lives in us. Our life belongs to Him. If your life is no longer your own, but His, then there is no room for fret or worry. Jesus surely knows what He wants to do and where He wants to go. Follow His lead and take comfort in Christ. Then remember that He is more than enough for whatever comes your way.

*Lord, thank You that my life is not my own, but Yours. I trust You today with all that is weighing on my heart. Amen.*

# A Strange Surrender

Jesus answered and said, "Permit even this."

**LUKE 22:51 NKJV**

---

Have you ever come face-to-face with a circumstance you really hoped to avoid? Or have you ever felt God leading you down a road with no clear destination in sight? When you don't understand what God is up to in your life, you can be encouraged by looking at Jesus in His dark hour of suffering.

Judas and the religious authorities arrived to arrest Jesus in the Garden of Gethsemane. As King of kings and Lord of lords, He could have commanded their death with one word. Instead, with a strange surrender and a heart fully abandoned to the will of His Father, He said to His disciples, "Permit even this."

When the Lord takes you in an unusual direction, don't resist, wrestle, or rebel. Instead, lean into His embrace, and whisper, "Permit even this." Heaven will tell the magnificent story of all that happens as a result.

*Help me, Lord, to have a willing heart today. Help me to say, "Yes, Lord, permit even this." Amen.*

# God Is in the Details

The LORD directs the steps of the godly.
He delights in every detail of their lives.

**PSALM 37:23 NLT**

How many times have you thought, *Lord, are You there? Do You care?* The amazing truth is that the God of creation cares about every detail of your life. He knows what you are facing, and He is with you, ready to strengthen you and support you. Knowing He is near, we can work without worry and rest in His love. Such is the ministry of His gracious promise for the steps of the godly.

Always remember that your Lord delights in you. Draw near to God today and delight in His care and compassion for you. Talk with Him about everything. He has a plan even for the small things because He delights in the details.

*Lord, thank You that You are God over the big things and the little things—every detail of my life. I rest in Your care, knowing I won't face anything today that escapes Your watchful eye and loving heart. Amen.*

# Why Not Trust?

I will trust in You.

**PSALM 55:23**

---------------------------------

Every day, moment by moment, you have two choices. You can trust in God, or you can worry about your circumstances. David experienced heart anguish, he was in fear for his life, and he was tempted to run away from the storm. But instead, he drew near to God, sat in God's presence, and reasoned through his trial. He asked God to hear his prayer. Then David acknowledged his many distractions and his own anxieties. Finally, he turned his attention to God's promises of salvation, redemption, peace, and deliverance. After his time with God, he found a new resolve—trust in God. He said, "I will trust in You."

Trust in God is a commitment of dependence and a belief in God's faithful provision for you. People who trust in God are able to Totally Rely Under Stress and Trial. They hold on to His promise to help in times of trouble. So today, why not choose to trust in God? Then eagerly watch to see what He will do.

*Lord, today I will trust in You. Amen.*

# Becoming a Friend of God

...Abraham My friend...

**ISAIAH 41:8**

--------------------------------

Abraham carries a distinguished title throughout the Old and New Testaments—he was God's friend. Imagine how you would feel if you heard God say, "You are my friend." Those would be the sweetest words for any believer to hear. One of the highest aspirations in any Christian's life is an intimate relationship with God and a real friendship with Him.

When you enjoy friendship with God, you experience His personal attention. He always invites His friends to join Him in His mission and plan (Genesis 12:1). God gives His friends His promises. He also shares His heart with His friends and constantly converses with them. God's friends enjoy His care and compassion. Finally, God commits Himself to His friends. You can count on Him and He counts on you.

Will you be God's friend today? Walk with Him as your best friend, and enjoy the fruit of a rich relationship with God.

*Lord, I want to take time to know You more and enjoy*
*a deep and vibrant friendship with You. Amen.*

# *Abba,* Father

You have received a spirit of adoption as sons
by which we cry out, "Abba! Father!"

**ROMANS 8:15**

A*bba.* This is the most precious, intimate name of God revealed to His children. *Abba* means Daddy or Papa and is an expression of endearment. It's an affectionate term used by small children for their fathers. As God's child, you have been granted the privilege of calling Him *Abba,* your Father. You are always welcome in heaven's throne room, where your heavenly Father is. You can run right into His presence and ask Him for whatever is on your heart. He expects you to be open, personal, bold, and courageous in His presence.

Friend, you have His smile. Don't be afraid, for He is your heavenly Father. He loves you. That's why the writer of Hebrews encourages us, "Let us draw near with confidence to the throne of grace, so that we may receive mercy and find grace to help in time of need" (Hebrews 4:16).

*Lord, thank You for the privilege of
calling You* Abba, *my Father. Amen.*

# Trusting *Abba*, Your Father

Abba! Father! All things are possible for You.

**MARK 14:36**

---

Tim Hansel writes about the time he and his son were climbing near some cliffs. Suddenly, Tim heard a voice above him yell, "Hey Dad! Catch me!" He turned just in time to see his son, Zac, gleefully jump off a rock and straight into his arms.

They both tumbled to the ground, and Tim gasped, "Zac! Can you give me one good reason why you did that?"

He calmly responded, "Sure...because you're my dad."

Zac boldly and joyfully lived life to the hilt because he knew he could trust his dad. In the same way, you can wholeheartedly trust your Father in heaven. Perhaps you see no way out of your trial and no clear answer for your need. When Jesus prayed to *Abba*, His Father, He knew the cross was before Him. And yet He trusted, saying "Abba! Father! All things are possible for You." You too can know all things are possible with your heavenly Father.

*Lord, I know all things are possible for*
*You, and I trust You today. Amen.*

171

# Finding Safety in God's Name

The name of the LORD is a strong tower;
The righteous runs into it and is safe.

**PROVERBS 18:10**

-------------------------------------------

The golf links at Turnberry, Scotland, feature small covered shelters at various areas on the course. Unless you actually play the course, you won't understand why those shelters exist. However, when you play golf at Turnberry, you experience their importance firsthand. During your golf round, you will undoubtedly watch dark clouds roll in and rain begin to fall. You look around, wondering what happened to your caddy. You then catch a glimpse of the caddy walking over the hill toward the shelter. He stands in the shelter, completely dry. You, of course, are soaking wet because you didn't know about the shelter.

Friend, did you know that you have a shelter in life? The Lord is your shelter, and when you run to Him, though the storm may rage, you are safe.

*Lord, thank You for being a strong tower,*
*where I can run when the storm clouds roll in. Amen.*

# The Power of God's Presence

The LORD is there.

**EZEKIEL 48:35**

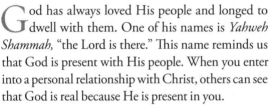

God has always loved His people and longed to dwell with them. One of his names is *Yahweh Shammah*, "the Lord is there." This name reminds us that God is present with His people. When you enter into a personal relationship with Christ, others can see that God is real because He is present in you.

Nicky Cruz was the leader of one of the most dangerous gangs in New York City. He was filled with violence and hate. One day he met Pastor David Wilkerson, who told him, "God has the power to change your life." Cruz hit Wilkerson and yelled at him. Wilkerson said, "You could cut me up into 1000 pieces and lay them in the street. Every piece would still love you." Cruz was struck with the presence of the Lord he witnessed in Wilkerson and eventually gave his life to Jesus.

Today, remember that *Yahweh Shammah* is at work, and others are seeing Him in your life.

*Lord, thank You for the power of Your presence. Amen.*

173

# When Life Is Upside-Down

*You meant evil against me, but God meant it for good in order to bring about this present result.*

**GENESIS 50:20**

---

Have you ever felt as though your life is upside-down? Joseph would certainly be able to relate. His brothers sold him to some Midianites, who took him to Egypt and sold him to Potiphar, one of Pharaoh's officers. Then he was thrown into prison when Potiphar's wife wrongly accused him of indiscretions. He found favor with the chief jailer but was forgotten by others whom he helped and who could have helped him. Even after more than two years in jail for no reason, Joseph continued to trust his sovereign God.

One day, God turned his life in a new direction. Joseph correctly interpreted Pharaoh's dreams and was suddenly promoted to the second-highest position in all of Egypt. Years later, when Joseph faced his brothers for the first time since they had sold him, he could have been bitter. Instead, he forgave and loved them.

When you are experiencing an upside-down life, remember that God is sovereign and is working out His plan.

*Lord, thank You for weaving my circumstances together in Your good plan and purpose. Amen.*

# The Help of the Lord

The LORD is my strength and my shield;
My heart trusts in Him, and I am helped;
Therefore my heart exults,
And with my song I shall thank Him.

**PSALM 28:7**

---

What happens when you trust in the Lord? He has promised that He will help you. When God says He will help, you can know you have all you need. He is the Father of mercies, the God of all comfort, the God of hope and grace, and so much more. Every one of God's names embodies a promise about Himself that He has given you. The Bible is filled with virtually thousands of promises about who God is, what He does, and what He says, so you are a spiritual multimillionaire. God's promises are like a bank account for you to draw on when the need arises. And surely you need Him now. Will you draw near and ask Him for His help?

*Lord, I need You now more than ever and call*
*upon You to help me in my time of trouble. Amen.*

# You Can Trust

How blessed is the man who has
made the LORD his trust.

**PSALM 40:4**

---

When Corrie ten Boom was a teenager, she witnessed the arrest and torture of another Christian. She was shocked and wondered how she could possibly endure such treatment. Running to her father, she sobbed, "I'm afraid I wouldn't be faithful."

He responded, "Corrie, God will give you the faith you need."

"I don't have that kind of courage and faith," she insisted.

Her father said, "Do you remember when you were a little girl and we took rides on the train? I kept your ticket in my pocket. Do you remember when I gave you your ticket?"

"Yes, right before we got on the train," she replied.

"Right," he said. "I kept it until you needed it so you wouldn't lose it. God will give you the faith you need. He will empower you by His Holy Spirit according to your need. Trust Him for that."

*Lord, today I trust You, knowing You will give
me what I need when I need it. Amen.*

# GROW

# God's Work in You

For I am confident of this very thing, that
He who began a good work in you will
perfect it until the day of Christ Jesus.

**PHILIPPIANS 1:6**

———————————————

*W*hat in the world is going on in my life? Have you ever entertained this thought or perhaps even spoken the words out loud? God answers your question in Paul's letter to the Philippian church. The Philippians needed encouragement and perhaps were questioning the whys of suffering—why me, why now, and why do we suffer at all?

God gives an encouraging word for all harrowing circumstances. He wants you to confidently know—without a doubt—that He has begun a good work in you and that He intends to complete what He has begun. Nothing, not even your present suffering, stands in His way. What happy news for you to know that God is working in you. And He is producing something good for His glory. Be encouraged by this one promise today in the midst of your difficult circumstance.

*Lord, thank You for beginning and completing*
*Your good work in me. Remind me of this promise*
*when I lose sight of my purpose in life. Amen.*

# God's Masterpiece

For we are God's masterpiece. He has created
us anew in Christ Jesus, so we can do the
good things he planned for us long ago.

**EPHESIANS 2:10 NLT**

-------------------------------

I f you ever have the opportunity to walk the streets of
Florence, Italy, you won't want to miss the Bargello
Palace. You will discover masterpieces by famous art-
ists like Michelangelo, Donatello, and Cellini.

Did you know that God has His own museum filled
with masterpieces? But His works of art are people. In
today's verse, you are called "God's masterpiece." Just
think, you are God's workmanship, sculpted by God
Himself. Earthly masterpieces are displayed in static
museums, but God's masterpieces don't sit in one place.
God's works of art join Him in doing good things He
planned for them long ago. People in the world watch
God's masterpieces in action. God is glorified, others
are drawn to Christ, and many are saved.

*Lord, help me understand my worth in You, that
I am Your magnificent masterpiece, created to do
good things You planned for me long ago. Amen.*

# Spiritual Growth

We are to grow up in all aspects into
Him who is the head, even Christ.

**EPHESIANS 4:15**

---

Have you ever held newborn babies and wondered at the intricate details of their hands or the precious features of their faces? And then you watch them grow from babies into young children, lanky teens, and then young adults. The physical and emotional changes demonstrate the mystery of the human growth process.

When you become a Christian and are born into the family of God, you embark on the journey of spiritual growth. When you grow spiritually, you become more and more like Christ in every way. God is at work in you, so you are becoming more than you are right now. Enjoy the process, dear friend, and watch in wonder as God grows you up in Christ.

*Lord, I'm excited to see You work in*
*me. I'm excited to grow up spiritually and*
*bring glory to Your name. Amen.*

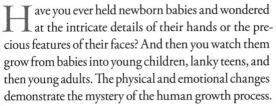

# How to Grow

Like newborn babies, long for the
pure milk of the word, so that by it you
may grow in respect to salvation.

**1 PETER 2:2**

-----------------------------------

Food is essential for physical growth. Similarly, spiritual food is necessary for spiritual growth. Your food to eat and beverage to drink is the Bible, God's Word. You need to long for God's Word like a newborn baby longs for milk. Have you watched newborns cry until they receive the sustenance they long for? You too must long for God's Word, hungrily eating it up and drinking it in. Then you will experience the satisfaction of a feast for your soul. Jeremiah described this feast when he said, "Your words were found and I ate them, and Your words became for me a joy and the delight of my heart" (Jeremiah 15:16).

Today, take time to acknowledge your need for sustenance from God's Word, open your Bible, and drink it in. Then grow, dear friend, as God intended when He saved you.

*Lord, thank You for the sustenance of Your Word
and the feast You have prepared for me. Amen.*

# God Causes the Growth

So then neither the one who plants nor the one who
waters is anything, but God who causes the growth.

**1 CORINTHIANS 3:7**

Spiritual masterpieces are never manufactured by
people or plans. Only God at work in the heart
causes spiritual growth. Remember that the best proce-
dures of man never match the transforming process of
God's Spirit in the heart. Though we plan and prepare,
we still need to rely on God to do the work. Methods
and strategies can point the way and provide a healthy
environment for spiritual growth. But in the end, as
Paul pointed out to the Corinthian church, God is the
One who makes men, women, and children more like
Christ. Never worship the method, only your Maker.
Don't surrender to strategies, only to God's Spirit.

Today, look to God for your growth in Christ. Ask
Him to do a mighty and powerful work in you.

*Lord, thank You for Your work in me. May
I stay surrendered to You so I can experience
Your transforming power. Amen.*

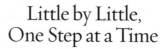

# Little by Little, One Step at a Time

*I will drive them out before you little by little, until you become fruitful and take possession of the land.*

**EXODUS 23:30**

---

Did you know that you can boil a cup of water in a microwave in less than a minute? Sometimes we expect spiritual growth will work the same way. Impatience sometimes rules the day, and we can become frustrated with ourselves. Maybe you've experienced impatience with your own spiritual progress. Remember, occasional joggers don't begin with a marathon. Hang in there, and keep on running your race, one step at a time. It's been said, "Inch by inch, it's a cinch. Yard by yard, it's hard."

Notice that God promised His people a land flowing with milk and honey. He did not fulfill His promise in a day; rather, the process took 40 years, for God knew fruitfulness in their lives required time to grow. And so it is with you. Spiritual growth takes time.

*Lord, help me run my race with faithfulness, little by little, one step at a time. Amen.*

# Fruit from the Vine

Every branch that bears fruit, He prunes
it so that it may bear more fruit.

**JOHN 15:2**

----------------------------

When you grow spiritually in Christ, you will bear spiritual fruit. How exciting to observe the work of God's Spirit in you! Your inner growth becomes evident on the outside. Others will see God's love, joy, peace, patience, kindness, and self-control in your life.

What does spiritual fruitfulness require? God prunes His vines so they may bear fruit. An untrimmed vine will develop long, rambling branches. Then very little fruit is produced because most of the strength of the vine is given to growing wood. Your Vinedresser wants His vine healthy and productive. Therefore, He prunes the branches, trimming them so they will bear more fruit. Recognize difficulties as tools God may be using in you to purge undetected areas of the self-life, like self-centeredness, self-sufficiency, and self-applause. Pruning is not glamorous, and it's often painful. Be encouraged today, knowing that God's pruning work is producing fruit.

*Lord, I can't wait to see Your fruit in my life. Amen.*

# Flourish Where
# You Are Planted

*Dwell in the land and cultivate faithfulness.*

**PSALM 37:3**

---

God sometimes plants His choice servants in strange lands. Some of the most magnificent works require extreme measures. God may place a juniper tree in the wilderness. Even in the deepest valleys, you can grow. God provides springs of water in the valleys. So regardless of where He plants you, dear friend, resolve to grow. Don't wait for a change in your circumstance. Instead, live in the land where God has placed you and cultivate faithfulness to Him. Amazingly, the very place you wanted to escape can become holy, sanctified, fertile soil. Fellowship with God can be sweetest in harsh lands, for He draws near to broken hearts and crushed spirits.

Hang in there, live in God's Word, walk and talk with Your Lord, and flourish in the land where God has placed you.

*Lord, thank You for this place where I am right now. Help me stand strong and live for You here. Be glorified in me today. Amen.*

# A Work in Process

For by that one offering He forever made
perfect those who are being made holy.

**HEBREWS 10:14 NLT**

---

Friend, take comfort in the fact that you have not yet arrived in your spiritual growth. You are a WIP—God's Work In Process. As a WIP, you can find joy in the moment, knowing you are right on schedule. You are not who you once were, and you are not yet who you will become in Christ.

Paul teaches a twofold view of sanctification, God's method of setting you apart for Himself. You are placed in Christ. In Him, you are forever made perfect. Your position in Him can never change, for He ensured your perfection through His death on the cross. Your life in Christ becomes a reality, little by little, as you spiritually grow. You are transformed within, made holy through the work of God's Spirit. Today, remember you are *in process* and rejoice at God's amazing plan for you.

*Lord, thank You for Your process*
*of making me holy. Amen.*

# Your New Identity

Paul and Timothy, bond-servants of Christ
Jesus, to all the saints in Christ Jesus who
are in Philippi…grace to you and peace from
God our Father and the Lord Jesus Christ.

**PHILIPPIANS 1:1-2**

Y ou have a high calling in God's kingdom. You are a
saint. God has forever changed your identity, making you holy, consecrated, and set apart. That's what it
means to be a saint.

Those who are meant to fly with wings of eagles cannot spend their time in the barnyard dirt of the world.
Saints can't live in the world's ways. Always remember
who you are as you go about the responsibilities in your
day. You are the Lord's saint. Understanding your identity does not make you arrogant, but gives you a true
focus on reality. Realizing your calling will help you
recognize God's choices for you. You will instantly see
the ways of the world are beneath one who belongs to
Christ. God will help you say no to many good things
in order to say yes to His best. So today, dear friend,
remember you are a saint.

*Lord, help me remember today that I am a saint. Amen.*

# Make the Most of Your Time

Therefore be careful how you walk, not as
unwise men but as wise, making the most
of your time, because the days are evil.

**EPHESIANS 5:15-16**

When you are a child, you want time to move fast so you can grow up. As an adult, you want time to slow down so you can savor each moment!

Use your time wisely, investing in spiritual, eternal things. When you invest your time in God and His Word, you are spending your time well. Giving time to people is also a wise choice. Think about how you are living your minutes and hours each day. Are you spending daily quiet time alone with God in His Word? Are you building godly relationships, investing in other people's lives so they can grow in Christ? The choices you make now will determine your stature in Christ ten years from now. So choose wisely, making the most of your time.

*Lord, help me make the most of my time today. Amen.*

# Give God Time

A thousand years in Your sight
Are like yesterday when it passes by.

**PSALM 90:4**

---

When God grows a squash, He takes a few months. But when God wants to make a magnificent oak tree, He takes much longer.

God takes His time when He grows you up spiritually in Christ. For Him, a thousand years are like a day. Saints in Christ need to trust God in their growth process. Surrender to God's timing, knowing God is carrying out His plan and purpose in your life. Lay aside your own ideas of timing, and persevere in His process. Your challenge is to live in the present in light of eternity.

C.S. Lewis pointed out that our discomfort with the passage of time indicates that we are creatures meant for eternity. The next time you wish the Lord would hurry and accomplish what you desire right now, remember He is working in you with eternity in His mind.

*Lord, I trust You today with the timing
of Your work in my life. Amen.*

# Seasons

For everything there is a season,
a time for every activity under heaven.

**ECCLESIASTES 3:1 NLT**

Just as there are seasons on the earth, so there are seasons of the soul. Spiritual growth occurs through all the seasons in your life. When you recognize your spiritual season, you will more easily trust God's work in you. Perhaps you are in a season of tears, mourning the loss of a loved one, a relationship, a home, or a job. God's presence is precious to those who are in a season of tears. Maybe you are in a season of productivity, responsible for an overwhelming array of jobs and people. You will learn steadfastness and faithfulness. In seasons of weakness, you learn how to rely on God for strength. In a season of joy, you cultivate gratefulness.

What season are you in, dear friend? Grow spiritually strong and tall in your season of life.

*Lord, thank You for this season of life. May I make the most of where I am and grow in You. Amen.*

191

# Press On to Maturity

Let us press on to maturity.

**HEBREWS 6:1**

---

Remember the first day you rode your bicycle without training wheels? You enjoyed a whole new freedom of movement. How about the day you earned your driver's license? That opened up yet another world of adventure. Who would ever want to go back to riding a bicycle with training wheels? And yet some Christians are still using training wheels when they should be driving a car.

The Lord encourages believers to press on to maturity, move forward in their growth, and go deeper into God's Word. You are not meant to be static, but to grow in your relationship with the Lord. You need to always move forward. Sometimes pressing on will mean following the Lord through pain, burdens, and other obstacles that threaten to stop you in your tracks. Never give up, dear friend. Press on to maturity.

*Lord, I want to move on with You and grow*
*deeper in my relationship with You. Amen.*

# Your Faith Can Grow

We hope that your faith will grow so that the
boundaries of our work among you will be extended.

**2 CORINTHIANS 10:15 NLT**

O n your spiritual growth journey, you may have
times when you feel as though you have a small
faith. You're in good company—the apostles felt that
way too (Luke 17:5). Never fear; your faith will grow.
God is in the business of growing and strengthening
your faith. In fact, faith is very much like a muscle that
grows with exercise. So just when you think your faith
is working overtime and is far too small, you are probably about to experience a faith growth spurt. Some
fitness trainers say, "No pain, no gain." When you exercise your faith in the pain and heartbreak of a trial,
you grow stronger in faith.

What will help your faith grow? Faith comes from
hearing the word of Christ (Romans 10:17). Your time
in God's Word will produce wonderful results, helping
you move from one level of faith to a new and stronger
expression (Romans 1:17). So today, take advantage of
every opportunity to grow in your faith.

*Lord, help me today to move from a*
*small faith to a great faith. Amen.*

# What Are You Thinking?

*Set your mind on the things above, not
on the things that are on earth.*

**COLOSSIANS 3:2**

-------------------------------

Do you ever find yourself in a time of spiritual lethargy or depression? Have you ever been so caught up in your circumstances that you became entangled in a net of negative thoughts? Where is your head these days? What are you thinking?

Paul encourages you to set your mind on the things above. He also invites you to take your mind off of things that are on earth. An eternal mind-set will propel you out of your spiritual discouragement. You will still deal with your difficulties, but your attitude will change. You have calculated God and His power into your situation. Now, your view of your life has an eternal perspective. And you glimpse what God can do. With your new vantage point, you are going to watch God accomplish a mighty work in your life.

*Lord, I need a heavenly mind-set today.
Help me look at life through Your eyes and
trust You with every detail. Amen.*

# Knowing Christ

Grow in the grace and knowledge of
our Lord and Savior Jesus Christ.

**2 PETER 3:18**

Peter offers a good way to measure spiritual growth. He encourages you to ask yourself, *Am I growing in the grace and knowledge of my Lord and Savior Jesus Christ?* First, how well do you know Him as Lord? When you know Christ as Lord of your life, you deny yourself, surrender to His ways, and follow Him.

Next, do you acknowledge Him as your Savior? So much is wrapped up in the name *Savior.* Jesus is your deliverer and preserver. He saves you from the danger of destruction and brings you to a happy, spiritually prosperous place. When you realize more and more about His nature as Savior, you will never run anywhere else for help or deliverance.

Finally, He is Christ, the Messiah. He is the fulfillment of all God's prophetic promises for forgiveness of sins and eternal life. Every day in your quiet time, ask, *What have I learned about Jesus today?*

*Lord, I want to know You more. Amen.*

# Spiritual Progress

*For if these qualities are yours and are increasing,*
*they render you neither useless nor unfruitful in*
*the true knowledge of our Lord Jesus Christ.*

**2 PETER 1:8**

-----------------------------------

How can a teacher know if a student is progressing? The best way is to give a test because examinations reveal how much you know and what you are learning.

Peter offers a compelling test to measure spiritual progress in 2 Peter 1:5-7. Think about these qualities and ask yourself, *How am I doing in my relationship with Christ?* Are you increasing in diligence, faith, moral excellence, knowledge, self-control, perseverance, godliness, brotherly kindness, and love? You may not be as mature as you'd like, but have you come a long way from where you were? Then rejoice, dear friend, for you are an instrument in the Lord's hand, and you are bearing fruit for the kingdom of God.

*Lord, thank You for giving me a tangible*
*measure of spirituality. I want to grow more*
*and more and give You all the glory! Amen.*

# Keep Running Your Race

Let us run with endurance the
race that is set before us.

**HEBREWS 12:1**

---

The race you are running with Jesus is unique, custom designed just for you. You may be thinking, *If only I could get rid of some of the distractions in my life, I could run my race. If God would change my circumstances, I could function so much better.* Friend, you need to know that the very thing you want to escape is part of your race. God is not worried that you won't make it. He is giving you strength and growing you spiritually so you can finish the race. You have need of endurance, so hang in there, keep on running, and never give up. Your race is before you. Keep running. Don't stop. Someday you will be thankful, for you will stand before your Lord, look Him in the eyes, and experience His smile and favor. Then you will know it was worth it all.

*Lord, help me keep on running the
race You've set before me. Amen.*

# Crossing the Finish Line

Do you not know that those who run in a
race all run, but only one receives the prize?
Run in such a way that you may win.

**1 CORINTHIANS 9:24**

---

T homas Huxley was in a hurry to catch a train. Step-
ping into a horse-drawn taxi in Dublin, he urged the
driver, "Hurry, I'm late. Drive fast!" The horses lurched
forward and galloped off. But when Huxley glanced
out the window, he realized they were going the wrong
direction! The scholar shouted, "Do you know where
you are going?"

Without looking back, the driver yelled back, "No,
your honor, but I'm driving very fast!"

So many are just like that taxi driver. They run fast,
but they are aimless. In order to win your race, you must
run with purpose and intention. When you run to win,
you will be thrilled at your reward.

*Lord, help me run my race with purpose and*
*intention so that I may win the prize. Amen.*

# REVIVE

# Personal Spiritual Revival

I am exceedingly afflicted;
Revive me, O LORD, according to Your word.

**PSALM 119:107**

R eal revival is personal and spiritual. The message from God is clear, especially in Psalm 119—He wants to revive your heart.

Psalm 119 is a sermon on revival. The psalmist is suffering and knows where to run in his difficulty. He cries out to God with a prayer every believer needs to memorize and pray, moment by moment: *Revive me, O Lord.* Oh, what a prayer this is for you today, dear friend. Are your heart and soul in trouble? Are you tired or worn out from a complex challenge in your job or home life? Personal revival is your greatest need. When God revives you, He quickens your heart and soul, imparting whatever is necessary to sustain your spiritual life and enable you to return to God's purpose for your life. Draw near to God today and pray for what you really need—personal, spiritual revival.

*Lord, revive me today. Revive me, O Lord. Amen.*

# Like a Wineskin in the Smoke

I am shriveled like a wineskin in the smoke.

**PSALM 119:83 NLT**

------------------------------

Fiery trials burn hearts, parch souls, and dry up people's passion. Like a wineskin in the smoke, the suffering one feels shriveled and shaken. Have you ever felt overcome with the heat and wondered how you would make it through? Take heart, dear friend, for a promise remains for all who suffer. When you pray, *Revive me, O Lord,* God pours His comfort and loving-kindness into your heart. He will give you just the right words in His Word, restoring your soul and enabling you to face another day. Just when you think you can't go on, grab your lifeline—God's Word—and you will experience inner deliverance from a thousand and one fears.

So don't be daunted by the smoke of your own weariness. You will be amazed how God can revive you even when you think revival is impossible. Nothing is impossible with God.

*Lord, revive me today and renew my*
*shaken, shriveled heart. Amen.*

# Like a Lost Sheep

I have wandered away like a lost sheep;
come and find me,
for I have not forgotten your commands.

**PSALM 119:176 NLT**

---

Y ou know those days when you feel lost in life? You wonder, *How did I arrive at this place?* Suddenly, you feel distant from God and alone, without a friend in the world. You long for even a drop of kindness. The psalmist prayed, "I have wandered away like a lost sheep; come and find me, for I have not forgotten your commands." He knew his only hope was the Lord. Only the Lord could find him and restore him.

And only the Lord can find you wherever you are, so call out to Him today. Pour out your heart to Him, telling Him your feelings and deepest longings. He is closer than you imagine, and He knows how to find you and restore you.

*Lord, at times I feel lost. Will you find me and*
*restore me to Your plan for me? Amen.*

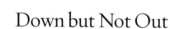

# Down but Not Out

I am worn out waiting for your rescue,
but I have put my hope in your word.
My eyes are straining
to see your promises come true.
When will you comfort me?

**PSALM 119:81-82 NLT**

---

Your wait for God's rescue may sometimes seem interminable. In fact, trials can last so long that eventually, no one offers you any more hopeful encouragement. Friend, when no one else has a promise for you, a promise remains in God's Word. You may be down, but you're not out. And though all others may have given up on you, God's presence with you is certain.

Nothing is impossible with God. And He gives you thousands of promises in His Word to revive your heart, giving you what you need to stand strong. So never give up, dear friend. God always keeps His promises. Longer waits often lead to greater rescues. You can count on God to come through and accomplish His rescue in His time.

*Lord, I am waiting for You, and today I*
*put my hope in Your Word. Amen.*

# The Secret of Revival

I lie in the dust;
revive me by your word.

**PSALM 119:25 NLT**

When the psalmist prayed for revival, he knew where to go to quench his deep thirst—God and His Word. Over and over again, he writes about the source of revival. He says, "This is my comfort in my affliction, that Your word has revived me" (Psalm 119:50). He prays, "Revive me by your word."

If you need revival today, open the pages of God's Word and live in each verse. God has given you the Bible, His love letter to you, to revive your heart. You may have thought your heart could never heal or find comfort. Take courage, for the Word of God restores hearts. Whatever your need today, your God has something specific to say to you. He wants to feed your needy soul. Ask Him to revive you, open your Bible, and discover God's nourishing, reviving words.

*Lord, thank You for the gift of Your reviving,*
*nourishing, healing, and comforting Word. Amen.*

# Are You Thirsty?

*If anyone is thirsty, let him come to Me and drink.*

**JOHN 7:37**

---

Jesus knows the thirst welling up in your heart. Two thousand years ago He cried out to the restless crowd, "If anyone is thirsty, let him come to Me and drink." He invites you today to come to Him and drink. How can you drink deeply of Him? Open your Bible, ask God to speak to you, and then slowly read what He says in His Word. Amazingly, you will notice certain verses as you read. Stop and think about what you are reading. Talk with God about the meaning of His Word.

When you come to God's Word, you are coming to the Lord Himself. Behind the written Word is the triune God, who spoke all things into existence (Hebrews 1:1-3; 2 Peter 1:20-21). When you drink His living water, you will be satisfied. Only the Lord's living water can quench thirsty hearts. So drink deeply today, dear friend.

*Lord, I'm thirsty today. Speak to me*
*from Your living Word. Amen.*

# Rivers of Living Water

He who believes in Me, as the Scriptures
said, "From his innermost being will
flow rivers of living water."

**JOHN 7:38**

------------------------------

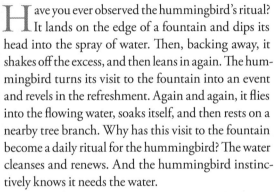

Have you ever observed the hummingbird's ritual? It lands on the edge of a fountain and dips its head into the spray of water. Then, backing away, it shakes off the excess, and then leans in again. The hummingbird turns its visit to the fountain into an event and revels in the refreshment. Again and again, it flies into the flowing water, soaks itself, and then rests on a nearby tree branch. Why has this visit to the fountain become a daily ritual for the hummingbird? The water cleanses and renews. And the hummingbird instinctively knows it needs the water.

Have you discovered that you need Jesus' living water? He promises rivers of living water for any person who believes in Him. When the rivers flow, you are renewed and refreshed. Come to Jesus today and experience the refreshing rivers of living water.

*Lord, let the rivers of living water*
*flow within me today. Amen.*

# The Spirit of Revival

But this He spoke of the Spirit, whom those
who believed in Him were to receive.

**JOHN 7:39**

---

The power behind personal revival is the Holy Spirit. He is the One who revives your heart and causes rivers of living water to flow in you. Think about the power of an electric power station. If all its power were used in one surge, entire neighborhoods would burn down. To prevent that, transformers break down the electricity into meaningful units. Similarly, the Holy Spirit gives you exactly what you need when you need it—truth from God's Word, God's love and comfort, strength in your weakness, and so much more. The Spirit's rivers of living water never stop flowing from within. Because Jesus has given you the indwelling Holy Spirit, you never run out of inner resources.

What is your need today? Do you need wisdom for a decision or strength in your job? Run to Jesus and ask for rivers of living water to flow in you through the Holy Spirit.

*Lord, thank You for the power of the Holy Spirit. Amen.*

# The Gift

You will receive the gift of the Holy Spirit.

**ACTS 2:38**

------------------------------------

When God gives gifts to His children, He includes many unexpected benefits. The Holy Spirit is one of your greatest gifts from God, and you need to unwrap this gift every day. Even though you cannot physically see the Holy Spirit, you can certainly observe His influence in your life.

When you need strength, run to the Holy Spirit and receive His power. When you feel you can't accomplish a task, run to the Holy Spirit and ask for His help. When you face angry and hurtful people, ask the Holy Spirit to give you His love. When you are in despair, ask Him for the joy of the Lord. When your life is filled with turbulence, run to Him for peace. Day after day, moment by moment, the Holy Spirit is more than equal to your greatest need. So pull off the bow and unwrap God's amazing gift to you today.

*Lord, thank You for the Holy Spirit. Help me rely on Him for every need in my life today. Amen.*

# The Secret of
# the Abundant Life

I came that they may have life,
and have it abundantly.

**JOHN 10:10**

-------------------------------

Have you ever heard the song from the late '60s "Is That All There Is?" What hopeless and depressing words! Jesus reaches out to searching, disillusioned people and sets the record straight about life. He promises abundant life for all who come to Him. You are designed to flourish and thrive in Him.

The problem is that often His children look for life in all the wrong places. Instead of living in fellowship with Jesus, walking and talking with Him, some have ventured far off the path God intended for them. Many have tried to find meaning and purpose in money, possessions, success, or earthly relationships. All of those things can change in a moment and leave people plunging into one crisis of the heart after another. Real life, abundant life, is found only in Jesus. So today, dear friend, walk with Him and talk with Him throughout your day.

*Lord, I come to You today and rely on You for the*
*abundant life that only You can give. Amen.*

# Sanctuary in a Scorched Place

The LORD will continually guide you,
And satisfy your desire in scorched places.

**ISAIAH 58:11**

God can turn scorched places into sanctuaries. He can dramatically alter seemingly impossible situations. How does He paint new landscapes in your trials? He never leaves you, never stops working, and continually guides you, even when you don't realize His presence in your life. He ultimately becomes your sanctuary, giving you His care and compassion. He knows you and communes with you in the depth of your being, where no one else has ventured. There, in your heart, reside your deepest desires. He promises in Isaiah 58:11 to meet these desires. He is creative in His provision, meeting you through a friend's encouragement, the words in the Bible, or even a surprise gift.

Eagerly anticipate God's work in you in the heat of a trial. You can face your darkest days with confidence, assured that One greater than yourself is watching over you.

*Lord, thank You for Your watchful eye
upon me, Your careful guidance, and Your
compassionate provision. Amen.*

# At the End of Your Rope

The Lord will…give strength to your bones.

**ISAIAH 58:11**

---

Have you been worn down by the scorched places in your life? God will meet you there. Have you been at the end of your rope with barely enough strength to hang on? God will meet you there and give you strength to persevere. Wherever you are, in any situation, He will "give strength to your bones." Sometimes even your bones ache from fatigue or illness. God knows about that too, and He promises His strength in your weakness.

God's strength far surpasses all earthly power and provision. You may be tempted to give up in your scorched place, feeling as though you have no hope. Grab hold of God's promises and find new inner strength to meet your challenge. Even when you don't feel God's strength, you can know that He is empowering you, and He is more than enough for your need today.

*Lord, I am holding my hand out now to*
*You, reaching beyond my own strength to*
*grasp Your abundant power. Amen.*

# Watered Gardens in Dry Places

And you will be like a watered garden,
And like a spring of water whose waters do not fail.

**ISAIAH 58:11**

---

One of the most beautiful sites in Paris is Les Tuileries garden, connecting the Louvre museum to the Arc de Triomphe on a straight line through the Champs-Élysées and Concorde square. The beautiful lawn, filled with flowers and fountains and statues, stretches a great distance along the Seine River. Chairs along various paths beckon visitors to take time for reflection and peace in the lush park environment.

God has fashioned an even more magnificent garden in your own heart. He has included a perpetual inner fountain of water and tends to your heart's growth Himself. Even when you walk through the hot wilderness of a devastating trial, you can experience a refreshing spa for your soul. Sit for a while in God's presence and enjoy His peace in His garden in your heart.

*Lord, I look forward to sitting with You
in Your garden in my heart. Amen.*

# Retreat to Revive

After He had sent the crowds away, He went
up on the mountain by Himself to pray; and
when it was evening, He was there alone.

**MATTHEW 14:23**

---

Sometimes you need to step away from the crowd to refuel and reenergize. Jesus knew the importance of time alone with God, especially in the midst of a busy, active ministry. He was intentional about retreating from people to be revived with His Father. He sent the crowds away, climbed a mountain alone, and stayed long into the night. He gives a wonderful example for all to follow. Step away from the crowd, find a quiet location conducive for prayer, and retreat to revive. Your heart will thank you for your courageous action of retreating with God. You need God's gracious encouragement more than you realize.

Jesus came down from the mountain and one day later was healing the sick and reasoning with the Pharisees. You also will emerge recharged and ready to face another day.

*Lord, thank You that I can retreat with You*
*and You will revive my heart. Amen.*

# Pursuing God

You who seek God, let your heart revive.

**PSALM 69:32**

Don't be surprised by the amazing way that God changes your character when you seek Him. Seeking God means you actively pursue Him with great care and concern. You long to know Him more. And so you spend more time with Him in His Word and in prayer. When you devote yourself to pursuing God, your life will change. You will want to open the Bible and read it more. You will long to serve the Lord with your gifts and talents. You will remember to pray at opportune moments. And you will begin to notice areas in your life that need to change.

Do you know what you're experiencing? Revival—personal, spiritual revival! When the Holy Spirit works in you, He transforms your heart, making you more like Christ. Sometimes His work will feel like house-cleaning. Other times, He will give you the sense that the windows have been opened and a cool, fresh breeze is blowing through your soul.

*Lord, let my heart revive today. Amen.*

# The Other Side of Trouble

You who have shown me
Many troubles and distresses
Will revive me again.

**PSALM 71:20**

When you know that every dark night leads to morning light, you find strength to endure in the midst of difficulties. You can know that revival from God is on the other side of all trouble and distress. God promises to revive you again and again. Revival comes by means of a perpetual fountain of living water through the Holy Spirit, who never stops working in you. You may be assured that even when you think life is at an end, a new day for you is around the corner.

In your trouble, look to the promise of inner transformation, soul restoration, and heart refreshment. Endure in the present trial, but keep an eye on the future fulfillment of God's Word in your life. Then you will experience strength to make it through to the other side.

*Lord, thank You for Your promise of*
*revival on the other side of every trouble*
*and distress. Revive me again. Amen.*

# At the Heart of Prayer

Revive us, and we will call upon Your name.

**PSALM 80:18**

---

We often think that if we work harder at devotion, we will become more spiritual. But the opposite is true. Spirituality is not what you do for God, but what He does in you. God is the One who revives your heart and draws you to Himself. Your prayer life grows in direct proportion to the Spirit's work of personal revival in you. When God produces streams of living water that flow in your heart, you will be filled with a new desire to talk with Him.

So, what will help you experience the reviving work of the Holy Spirit? Give the Spirit plenty of kindling for the spiritual fire He is tending in your heart. Stay in God's Word, drink it in, and think often about what you read in the Bible. Your heart may be dry, but the wind of the Holy Spirit is strong, and the Word of God is sure and steady.

*Lord, revive my heart and lead me*
*deeper in prayer. Amen.*

# Run Before the Wind

Men spoke from God who were borne along
(moved and impelled) by the Holy Spirit.

**2 PETER 1:21 AMP**

---

The nautical term *bear away* means to change a ship's course so it can run before the wind. The position of the sail determines its ability to catch the wind. When the sail reaches the correct position and catches the full force of the wind, the ship sails smoothly.

What a joy to watch sailboats gliding on the water with the power of the wind propelling them forward. And how wonderful to see believers respond to the power of the Holy Spirit blowing through their lives! Sometimes the Spirit of God moves in a new direction. Instead of wrestling with His move, surrender and set your sail to catch the new direction of the wind. Whatever you may be experiencing today, recognize God's Spirit at work in you. Surrender and then run before the wind.

*Lord, may I run before the wind of Your Spirit
today and sail on the ocean of Your love. Amen.*

# What Moves God's Heart

If my people, who are called by my name, will humble
themselves and pray and seek my face and turn
from their wicked ways, then will I hear from heaven
and will forgive their sin and will heal their land.

**2 CHRONICLES 7:14 NIV**

---

King Solomon prayed a heartfelt prayer to God during the dedication of the temple. He asked God whether His people could enjoy life with Him even in dark times. Do you ever wonder the same thing? When life seems impossible, do you wonder if your relationship with God will prevail and make a difference?

You need to know that your difficult circumstances and your needs form the platform for God's reviving work in your life. Solomon prayed his prayer in public but received God's response in private. God personally draws near to individuals who truly desire to hear from Him. God is moved when you humble yourself and lay out your need before Him. He told Solomon that if His people would humble themselves, turn away from their wicked ways, and seek Him, He would hear from heaven and heal their land. Today, lay your heart out before the Lord and watch in anticipation for His response.

*Lord, thank You for responding
when I cry out to You. Amen.*

# The Humble Heart

If my people, who are called by my
name, will humble themselves...

**2 CHRONICLES 7:14 NIV**

Personal revival begins with God. It continues with your intentional response. God revives humble hearts. He is looking for those who are absolutely dependent upon Him, overwhelmed with a sense of personal need, and longing for a fresh encounter with God. The Lord wants you to sense your need and run to Him. He is blessed when you fall at His feet, realizing your own weakness and sin. He loves your worship when you recognize His goodness and glory. Your humility is a living reflection of the Lord Jesus in you because the Lord's heart is a humble heart. The humble heart turns to God, and He touches and moves and changes it.

Don't be afraid to choose the low place or seem unimportant in other people's eyes. Choose to be famous in God's secret audience. Always remember that the humble heart is the revived heart.

*Lord, weave humility into my character today*
*and help me shine for You in the world. Amen.*

# Responding to God's Word

If my people...turn from their wicked ways...

**2 CHRONICLES 7:14 NIV**

God always expects action when He speaks. He told Solomon that the people must turn from their wicked ways. Whenever God sends out His Word, He expects it to transform people. He says, "My word... will not return to Me empty, without accomplishing what I desire, and without succeeding in the matter for which I sent it" (Isaiah 55:11). When God revives you, He moves your heart to respond to His Word. Your obedient response is evidence of the Spirit's transforming work in you.

Every day you are faced with opportunities to live out God's Word in obedience to Him. Your convictions and resolutions, based on what you have learned in the Bible, will help you obey God. What response is God seeking in you today? Determine to say yes to God and enjoy His transforming work in your life.

*Lord, revive me and move my heart to*
*respond to Your Word today. Amen.*

# What Happens When God Hears?

Then will I hear from heaven and will
forgive their sin and will heal their land.

**2 CHRONICLES 7:14 NIV**

When God revives your heart, He restores and strengthens you with everything you need to walk with Him. In other words, He gives you what you need to carry on in life.

Revival comes in many forms. Revival may mean forgiveness of sin, strength in weakness, a change in attitude, love for an enemy, an idea for ministry, or wisdom in a difficult situation. Whenever the Lord works in your heart and in your life, you experience His reviving touch through the power of the Holy Spirit. That's why personal revival is absolutely necessary in your normal experience with God. Personal revival is not elusive or optional; it's vital if you are to participate in God's plan and purpose.

Prepare yourself for God's surprises. He may choose to use you in great and mighty ways for His glory.

*Lord, revive me and use me today
for Your great glory. Amen.*

# The First Thing

*I urge you, first of all, to pray for all people.*

**1 TIMOTHY 2:1 NLT**

---

Joseph Scriven wrote the beloved hymn "What a Friend We Have in Jesus" to comfort his mother. He encouraged her and all believers to pray when he wrote, "O what peace we often forfeit, / O what needless pain we bear, / All because we do not carry / Everything to God in prayer." Have you known his words to be true? Prayer is often our last resort rather than our first response.

S.D. Gordon says, "There are people that put prayer first, and group the other items in life's schedule around and after prayer. These are the people who are doing the most for God." Prayer is your primary occupation and vocation. It's not an afterthought, but the main thought. We pray first because of the urgency of the hour, the clear priority of prayer, and the tremendous need for prayer for all people. Today, whatever else you do, first of all, pray.

*Lord, help me to always pray first*
*in every situation. Amen.*

# The Life of Prayer

Never stop praying.

**1 THESSALONIANS 5:17 NLT**

----

Prayer is more than a single request to God. Prayer is a life; it is an intimate, ongoing, vibrant relationship with God that is nurtured through specific times alone with Him. Prayer is walking and talking with God.

Imagine some of your best conversations with a friend. You both share your thoughts, feelings, and ideas. You never just sit and constantly ask for everything you want. In your conversation with God, always pour out your heart to Him. He is interested in the details. Share your joys, sorrows, hopes, and dreams. Moses enjoyed this kind of intimate conversation with God. The Lord spoke with Moses "face to face, just as a man speaks to his friend" (Exodus 33:11).

Cultivating your life of prayer will require time and intention. Intimate communion with God doesn't simply materialize out of thin air. Today, take time to walk and talk with God, just as you would with your dearest friend.

*Lord, thank You for desiring constant*
*conversation and communion with me. Amen.*

# God's Prescription for Worry

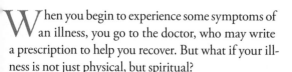

Don't worry about anything; instead,
pray about everything.

**PHILIPPIANS 4:6 NLT**

------------------------------------

When you begin to experience some symptoms of an illness, you go to the doctor, who may write a prescription to help you recover. But what if your illness is not just physical, but spiritual?

One of the first symptoms of spiritual trouble is worry. Our hearts tend to react to adverse circumstances with anxiety. We mull over all the possible worst-case scenarios before anything has even happened. Have you noticed that most of your worries never actually materialize? Worry wastes precious time. No wonder God says, "Don't worry about anything."

God's prescription for worry is prayer. Prayer does not always come naturally in the midst of a difficult situation. We panic more easily than we pray. But thankfully, you can count on the Spirit of God to prompt you to pray. Somewhere in the midst of your trial, you will remember God and turn your heart toward Him. If you will resolve in advance of troubles to pray instead of worry, you will more likely run to God in the heat of the moment.

*Lord, help me always choose prayer over worry. Amen.*

# The Two Sides of Prayer

Tell God what you need, and thank
him for all he has done.

**PHILIPPIANS 4:6 NLT**

When you enter into a conversation with God, what will you say? Paul outlines the most important elements in any conversation with the Lord—requests and thanksgiving. The very essence of your prayer is worship and devotion. When you walk and talk with God, your heart assumes a reverent position. You realize God's majesty, breathe in the heavenly atmosphere of His throne room, and humbly bow at His feet. Then you can converse with your Lord.

The Lord loves you, so tell Him all your heartfelt needs. Asking God to help you is one side of prayer. Thanking God is the other side of prayer. Thanksgiving helps you remember God's work in the past so you can believe Him in the present. Spend time today sharing your needs with God and thanking Him for all He has done in your life.

*Lord, I come to You now with my deepest needs and*
*thanksgiving for all You have done for me. Amen.*

# Jesus, Your Prayer Partner

I have prayed for you.

**LUKE 22:32**

---

W hen you are in trouble, you need someone to come alongside and pray for you. You can be encouraged today because you have the most reliable prayer partner anyone could imagine—Jesus Himself. Jesus knew Peter was about to endure one of his darkest hours. What did He do about the pending trial? He prayed for Peter that his faith would not fail.

Peter never could have prayed that prayer, for he did not even know his own need. Similarly, you don't always know what to pray or how to pray. But Jesus knows, and He will pray for you. He "always lives to make intercession" for you (Hebrews 7:25). Your prayer partner, Jesus, is able to sympathize with your weaknesses, and He knows your distresses and adversities. He knows you completely and wholeheartedly loves you. If you have trusted Jesus to save you, you can certainly rely on Him now to pray for you.

*Lord, thank You for coming alongside me and*
*praying for me in my time of need. Amen.*

# The Holy Spirit, Your Prayer Partner

The Spirit also helps our weakness; for we do not know how to pray as we should, but the Spirit Himself intercedes for us…He intercedes for the saints according to the will of God.

**ROMANS 8:26-27**

W hen you feel weak in prayer, you can trust your prayer partner, the Holy Spirit, to help you. You may feel weak in prayer because you are battling illness or even spiritual warfare against the enemy (Ephesians 6:12). Or you may find yourself entrenched in extreme adversity. You may not even know your own needs. Sometimes only God knows your heart and understands the solution.

When you know Christ, you can trust the indwelling Spirit of God to help you in your weakness. He intercedes for the saints, and He always knows your needs and prays according to God's will. The next time you feel weak in prayer, you can have confidence because of your intercessor, the Holy Spirit.

*Lord, thank You for anticipating my need for the Holy Spirit, who prays for me according to Your will. Amen.*

# The Psalmists, Your Prayer Partners

On the day I called, You answered me.

**PSALM 138:3**

Have you ever longed for someone to show you how to pray? God anticipated your need for prayer examples and gave you the psalms. The psalmists knew how to pray and are wonderful prayer partners for you. When you open to any psalm in the Bible and pray the words, you will experience a lesson on prayer. The psalmists show you how to worship and praise, thank God, confess sin, and ask God for help. Read the psalms and write out everything you learn about prayer. You will be surprised at the length of your list.

Just think about the caliber of people who will teach you. The psalmists include David, Moses, Asaph, King Solomon, and the sons of Korah. What a privilege you have today to enter into the school of prayer in the psalms.

*Lord, teach me more about prayer as I read
and pray through the psalms. Amen.*

# The Power of Praise

Sing praise to the LORD, you His godly ones,
And give thanks to His holy name.

**PSALM 30:4**

---

Praise has the power to pull you out of the pits. David encouraged those around him to sing praises to the Lord and give thanks to His holy name. David explained, "weeping may last for the night, but a shout of joy comes in the morning" (Psalm 30:5). Praise turns the tide of trouble in your soul. Just when you feel as though despair will overtake you, praise brings a wave of joy into your heart. Joy is not the absence of suffering, but the presence of God.

How can you possibly sing praises when your heart is heavy? Open the Bible to the psalms and begin living there. Read a favorite psalm out loud in the presence of your Lord. Turn the words to prayer, and you will soon enter into praise and thanksgiving.

*Lord, lead me into praise and thanksgiving, so
I can shout with joy in the morning. Amen.*

# When You Sin

If we confess our sins, He is faithful and
righteous to forgive us our sins and to
cleanse us from all unrighteousness.

**1 JOHN 1:9**

Have you ever carried the weight of sin and longed to feel the heaviness of guilt lift off your heart? Jesus died on the cross that you might be forgiven of all your sin—past, present, and future. The answer for your need when you sin is confession.

Confession means simply to agree with God that you have sinned. John said that if you confess your sins, God is faithful to forgive and cleanse you. When you confess your sins, you experience God's forgiveness. And "there is now no condemnation for those who are in Christ Jesus" (Romans 8:1). You are set free because the blood of Christ was shed on your behalf. Keep short accounts with God. When you become aware of a sin, immediately confess it and then enjoy blessed fellowship with your Lord.

*Lord, today I confess my sin to You. Thank*
*You for Your forgiveness. Amen.*

# A Model of Confession

Against You, You only, I have sinned.

**PSALM 51:4**

---

David stood on the roof of his house one evening and noticed Bathsheba, his neighbor's wife. He slept with Bathsheba and thought his sin would remain secret. Then he received Bathsheba's message: "I am pregnant." David tried to cover up his sin, and it grew from adultery to deception and murder. Sin always entices with false promises, and then it multiplies. When David finally realized he had sinned against God, his heart was broken. He changed his futile direction and ran into God's presence in prayer. He took his sin before a just and holy God and became a model of confession for all who would be free of the weight of unconfessed sin.

Confess your sin today and experience God's forgiveness. Remember Corrie ten Boom's words: "When we confess our sins, God casts them into the deepest ocean, gone forever. Then God places a sign out there that says No Fishing Allowed."

*Lord, help me bring every sin to You. Thank You for Your mercy, grace, and forgiveness. Amen.*

# When Your Eyes Go Bad

When I pondered to understand this,
It was troublesome in my sight
Until I came into the sanctuary of God;
Then I perceived their end.

**PSALM 73:16-17**

-------------------------------------

Asaph had a problem with spiritual eyesight, and you may be able to relate. He took off his spiritual glasses and began looking at life with his physical eyes. Leaning on his own understanding, he saw only prosperity and ease for the wicked and arrogant. Asaph fell into a sea of envy and bitterness and wondered why he should remain pure and innocent if his lifestyle led only to suffering.

Have you ever fallen into the trap of looking at life through your own eyes? Realize, as Asaph did, that your eyes have gone bad, and you need help. Asaph ran to God in prayer. Prayer takes you into God's sanctuary and restores your spiritual vision. After entering the sanctuary, Asaph saw the vanity of godless living and the glorious future for those who follow the Lord. Run to God today to maintain your spiritual eyesight.

*Lord, help me look at all of life through Your eyes. Amen.*

# Prayer Outside the Box

I pray You, show me Your glory!

**EXODUS 33:18**

----

Moses enjoyed perhaps one of the most intimate, engaging relationships with God described in the Bible. God spoke with Moses face-to-face, just as a man speaks to his friend (Exodus 33:11). They shared their hearts with one another candidly. Because of this close relationship, Moses was not afraid to talk with God. His boldness arose out of a committed, humble heart for God (Numbers 12:3). He simply loved God, and God loved him.

One day, Moses took his prayer outside the boundaries of anything he had ever requested. He prayed, "Show me Your glory!" God so loved Moses' prayer that He revealed the brightness of His blazing glory just long enough to give Moses a glimpse. But a glimpse of glory was enough for a lifetime. Today, pray outside the box—ask God that you may know Him more and catch a glimpse of His glory.

*Lord, I long to know You more and*
*to behold Your glory. Amen.*

# Pouring Out Your Soul

I have poured out my soul before the LORD.

**1 SAMUEL 1:15**

---

When your soul is in distress, think about Hannah. Usually distress comes from wanting what you don't have or having what you don't want. In Hannah's case, she longed for a child. And yet year after year, she was barren. Her rival, Peninnah, had many children and loved to provoke Hannah. Although Hannah's husband loved her, he grew tired of her sorrow: "Am I not better to you than ten sons?"

Perhaps some distressing situation has left you feeling the way Hannah did. Maybe your heart is broken and no one understands or offers you kindness. Learn to take your distress to the Lord. Hannah entered the temple and wept, pouring her soul out to the Lord. Her precious prayer time renewed her heart. God responded to her prayer, and she conceived and gave birth to Samuel, the Lord's prophet who anointed David as king.

When you are in distress, remember Hannah and pour out your soul to the Lord.

*Lord, You know the sorrows I carry in my heart.*
*Address them today in Your loving-kindness. Amen.*

# Prayer in the Depths

I waited patiently for the LORD;
And He inclined to me and heard my cry.

**PSALM 40:1**

---

You may feel as though you are trapped in an impossible circumstance. Like David, you may appear to be stuck in miry clay with no way out. Have you prayed and prayed and then waited and waited for something to happen? Maybe you are wondering whether your prayers are even reaching God and whether He will answer.

David would be able to identify with your experience. He felt as though he was in the pit—stuck in mud and unable to move. He cried out to God but heard no answer. He was forced to wait, and his patient and prayerful waiting is the secret to prayer in the depths. Continue praying and waiting for God's response. He has already answered but has evidently attached a date to His response.

Our issue is that we want everything now. And if we don't see immediate resolution, we wrongly interpret God. Today, cry out to God and wait patiently and prayerfully for His response.

*Lord, thank You for hearing my cry. Amen.*

# Never Give Up

He was telling them a parable to show that at all
times they ought to pray and not to lose heart.

**LUKE 18:1**

When should you pray? According to Jesus, you should pray at all times and never lose heart. Jesus' words reveal that He sees and knows your heart. He knows your life is wrought with disappointing conditions that may discourage you from praying. He knows you will sometimes be tempted to lose heart when you pray. You too are well acquainted with your own tendency to give up. Maybe God hasn't worked in the way you expected, or He hasn't changed your circumstance immediately as you had hoped.

How will you handle this unexpected response from God? Keep praying and don't lose heart. Jesus spoke of a widow who persistently prayed and finally received her answer. Today, follow the widow's example—keep praying and never ever give up.

*Lord, I have presented my request to You. Thank
You for hearing me and encouraging me to
keep praying and not lose heart. Amen.*

# Spiritual Warfare

With all prayer and petition pray at all times in the
Spirit, and with this in view, be on the alert with
all perseverance and petition for all the saints.

**EPHESIANS 6:18**

---

You are a soldier of Jesus Christ, and one of your main duties is to pray. Oswald Chambers says, "Prayer does not equip us for greater works—prayer is the greater work." When Paul describes your spiritual battle, he encourages you to "put on the full armor of God, so that you will be able to stand firm." He lists two offensive weapons: the Word of God and prayer. Prayer is one of your most powerful weapons against your enemies—the world, the flesh, and the devil. Prayer is "divinely powerful for the destruction of fortresses" (2 Corinthians 10:4). God's power is unleashed against evil when you pray.

When the enemy tries to discourage or defeat you, start praying. Watch as God defeats every enemy and strengthens you in the battle.

*Lord, I pray for Your strength and power
in this spiritual battle. Amen.*

# Prayers of the Saints

Another angel came…and much incense was given
to him, so that he might add it to the prayers of all
the saints on the golden altar which was before
the throne. And the smoke of the incense, with
the prayers of the saints, went up before God.

**REVELATION 8:3-4**

G od gives us a graphic image of what happens when
we pray. Your prayers are always in God's presence.
In Revelation, your prayers are pictured as incense at
God's throne, with the smoke of the incense carrying
your prayers directly to God. You never need to wonder
whether your prayers are reaching heaven or having an
effect. Every time you speak with God, imagine your
words burning as perpetual incense in God's presence.
Prayer upon prayer continually reaches God, and He re-
sponds to each one. Knowing you have God's audience, you can confidently pray about everything. Then
relax in the assurance that He has heard and that He
will answer.

*Lord, I bring all my prayers to You today. Thank You*
*for hearing and answering every request. Amen.*

# Confident Prayers

This is the confidence which we have before
Him, that, if we ask anything according to His
will, He hears us. And if we know that He hears
us in whatever we ask, we know that we have
the requests which we have asked from Him.

**1 JOHN 5:14-15**

How can you become a more confident prayer warrior? Open God's Word and pray through each verse. If you ask God for anything according to His will, He hears you. Then He gives you confidence that He has answered your prayer. Your confidence depends on praying according to His will, and God's will is written across every page of the Bible, so if you want to pray according to God's will, pray God's Word.

For example, if you are in trouble, pray through Psalm 46:1: *Lord, You are a very present help in times of trouble. I ask You now to help me.* God promises His help and will respond to your cry.

*Lord, thank You for promising to hear and answer
when I pray according to Your will. Amen.*

# Waiting in Prayer

I wait for the LORD, my soul does wait,
And in His word do I hope.
My soul waits for the Lord
More than the watchmen for the morning.

**PSALM 130:5-6**

---

Waiting for God is a form of prayer. When you wait, you trust and quietly commune with God. You are still asking, but you haven't seen God's answer. You know you will see His answer in His time.

Sentries guarding the walls of a city know that day will eventually come. The sun may seem to tarry, but watchmen know it will soon rise. So too, your soul waits for your Lord. Though He may tarry, He will surely respond. When you wait, your prayer includes hope in God's Word. Fill your heart and mind with God's promises, and your prayers will soon display a new hope.

Perhaps you are waiting on God even now. You can know, as sure as the sunrise, you will receive God's answer.

*Lord, today I wait on You and hope in all
the promises of Your Word. Amen.*

# In Due Season

They all wait for You
To give them their food in due season.
You give to them, they gather it up;
You open Your hand, they are satisfied with good.

**PSALM 104:27-28**

-------------------------------

Every answer to prayer arrives "in due season." God gives you what you need according to His timetable, not yours. If you have not yet received your answer from God, you can know it's not yet due season. Earlier in the psalm, the psalmist demonstrates God's provision in all creation, in plants, and in animals. Just as God gives food to animals and rainfall for plants at the appropriate time, so too He will give you what you require at just the right time: in due season. When He provides, you will gather up His provision, receiving all you need, and you will be satisfied.

Think today about those prayers that still fill your heart. Wait for God with confidence, knowing His due season is yet to come.

*Lord, I am waiting for You and trust You to*
*provide all my needs in due season. Amen.*

# Do You Love Jesus?

*Simon, son of John, do you love Me?*

**JOHN 21:16**

---

Peter had denied Christ three times. Brokenhearted at his own failure, he ran away during his Master's darkest hour. But Jesus met him later after the resurrection and asked a very simple question: "Do you love Me?" Jesus wanted Peter to know that agape love for Him was at the heart of all ministry. He wants His disciples to be attached to Him exclusively, to love and follow Him at all costs.

Peter, grieved at his own lack of commitment, responded to Jesus' question with a different word for love, implying something like, "I love You like a friend." After Jesus repeated His question twice, Peter finally responded, "Lord, You know all things." Peter was saying, "Lord, You know my heart. I want to love You at all costs. But I'm weak and a failure." Jesus responded, "Tend My sheep" (John 21:17). His words assured Peter of His love and commitment to him. Today, be assured that Jesus loves you and wants you to serve Him.

*Lord, I'm aware I'm weak. Help me*
*to love You at all costs. Amen.*

# Serving the Lord

Tend My sheep.

**JOHN 21:17**

How many employers would hire someone who is weak and prone to failure? And yet this is exactly what Jesus did with Peter. When Peter finally agreed with Jesus that he could not love unconditionally, Peter enjoyed an authentic moment of intimacy with Jesus. Peter's soul was laid bare with a sense of raw openness. In those moments, Jesus knew He had Peter's heart. Jesus was not worried about Peter's immaturity, for He had taken him on as His disciple. He still wanted Peter to serve Him and knew his love would grow and mature. And so Jesus gave Peter beautiful words of assurance: "Tend My sheep." He was promising Peter that He had a future of service for him in His kingdom.

Perhaps you too are weak or have failed and have wrongly concluded that you can never serve Jesus again. Take heart, dear friend. Jesus loved Peter in spite of his failure, and He loves you also.

*Lord, thank You for Your love, which far surpasses my own weakness and failure. Amen.*

# The Power of Love

Love never fails.

**1 CORINTHIANS 13:8**

---

God's love is so powerful that it compelled Him to give Jesus, His beloved Son, to die on the cross for your sins. His love is the reason you can experience forgiveness of sins and eternal life. And now you have the opportunity to give His magnificent love to someone else. Love has the power to change impossible situations and people. God's love has revolutionized marriages and transformed hearts.

Someone in your life needs God's love today. Ask God to show you how to express His love to that person. Also, have you told those closest to you that you love them? You will be amazed at the results of a simple, heartfelt "I love you." Maybe you are living with difficult people. Have you told them lately that you love them? "I love you" builds bridges and heals relationships. Say those words today and watch what God does.

*Lord, help me give Your love away*
*to someone today. Amen.*

# The Great Commission

*All authority has been given to Me in*
*heaven and on earth. Go therefore…*

**MATTHEW 28:18-19**

---

When the famous English architect Sir Christopher Wren was directing the building of St. Paul's Cathedral in London, he oversaw a large crew of men. A journalist interviewed some of the workers. He asked some, "What are you doing here?" The first said, "I'm cutting stone for three shillings a day." The second replied, "I'm putting ten hours a day in on this job." The third replied, "I'm helping Sir Christopher Wren build the greatest cathedral in Great Britain for the glory of God." Each of these men clearly had different philosophies of service.

How do you view your ministry? What convictions stand behind your desire to serve the Lord? Jesus commissioned you when He said, "Go therefore…" Listen to His words and discover your reason for service. Ministry is not about killing time or earning money. You are in the service of the King of kings and Lord of lords.

*Lord, I am so proud and honored*
*to serve You today. Amen.*

# Why Should You Serve the Lord?

All authority has been given to Me
in heaven and on earth.

**MATTHEW 28:18**

---

Jesus can rightfully command your beliefs and actions, for He is God. How can you know what He desires for your life today? Simply open the pages of the Bible, the living and active Word of God (Hebrews 4:12). As you build a philosophy of ministry, first know that you serve the Lord because He has commissioned you into service. Jesus says, "All authority has been given to Me in heaven and on earth." You engage in ministry because Jesus is the One asking you to serve Him. Be clear about why you serve, and you won't give up on your ministry in the heat of a trial.

Whenever you feel discouraged about your service to the Lord, remember that Jesus is the One commissioning you into His work for the kingdom of God. You will find new strength to serve your Lord.

*Lord, thank You for commissioning*
*me into Your service. Amen.*

# Your Perspective in Ministry

Go therefore...

**MATTHEW 28:19**

---

Consider this unique perspective as you form your philosophy of ministry. You are God's pilgrim, and your home is in heaven. Therefore, you are on a journey with your Lord. People who travel this path don't sink their roots too deeply in earthly things. God may call you to something new.

Jesus commissioned His disciples to go. For them, *go* meant beginning the early church, which in turn meant that some would preach to thousands, some would travel from one area to another, and all would somehow give out the Word of God. Some of these disciples were God's first missionaries, spreading the gospel to the world.

For you, *go* means that you are to be open to any new area of service God may ask of you. Be prepared to say yes to God even though you may wrestle with His plan. Saying yes may mean that you step up to a new position you could never have imagined for yourself. Today, think about areas where you need to surrender so you can say yes to your Lord and go.

*Lord, today I am surrendered to follow*
*You wherever You may lead. Amen.*

# The Scope of Your Ministry

Make disciples of all the nations.

**MATTHEW 28:19**

---

What ideas do you have for ministry? Maybe you desire to reach out to needy people. Or perhaps you want to encourage men and women in assisted living or nursing homes. Have you considered leading a Bible study? Regardless of where you focus your ministry, always remember to include the world in your sights. Jesus invites you to include a worldwide vision in your philosophy of ministry when He says, "Go and make disciples of all the nations." He wants to use you to reach the world with the gospel.

How does He accomplish this amazing goal? Through a ripple effect of changed lives, one person at a time, your life can make a difference in the world. You will never see the thousands of lives you influence through your faithfulness to the Lord. But heaven will tell the story of the ripple effect of your life. So today, remember that God is using you in ways that extend beyond your corner of the world.

*Lord, thank You for Your worldwide*
*influence in and through me. Amen.*

# The Great Promise
# in Your Ministry

I am with you always, even to the end of the age.

**MATTHEW 28:20**

---

S ervice to the Lord includes many solitary moments. Much of your work for the Lord is behind the scenes. No one sees some of the most important parts of your ministry. You don't always receive applause or accolades. But Jesus promises that even though you feel alone during your brief stay on earth, you never really are. He will always be with you. Even when no one else sees your ministry, Jesus sees and knows. And heaven applauds God's work in and through you. Whether you are alone or in the company of thousands, you always serve in the audience of One, the Lord Jesus.

Be encouraged with Jesus as your constant companion. He is your strength, wisdom, comfort, sustenance, and security. Cultivate a sense of Jesus' presence in your life today. Enjoy His companionship, knowing He sees your service and supplies all your needs. When you have Jesus, you have all you need in ministry.

*Lord, thank You for Your presence*
*in my life and ministry. Amen.*

# Who Are Your Leaders?

Remember those who led you, who spoke
the word of God to you; and considering the
result of their conduct, imitate their faith.

**HEBREWS 13:7**

W ho are the leaders who have served as your examples and poured their lives into yours? Today's
verse encourages you to remember them and imitate
their faith. Remembering the leaders who have shaped
your life will encourage you, strengthen your commitment, and motivate you to follow their example.

Take a sheet of paper and make a list of those who
have been the most powerful examples for you. Write
out the most important things you learned from each
person. You may even want to write each name next to
Hebrews 13:7 in your Bible. Finally, talk with the Lord
and thank Him for each significant man or woman
who has taken you higher and deeper in your walk with
God. Read through Hebrews 13:7 again and ask yourself, *Who could write my name next to this verse?*

*Lord, thank You for all these Hebrews 13:7*
*men and women in my life. Make me*
*a Hebrews 13:7 woman. Amen.*

# The Essence of Ministry

*Thanks be to God, who always leads us in triumph
in Christ, and manifests through us the sweet
aroma of the knowledge of Him in every place.*

**2 CORINTHIANS 2:14**

Billy Graham issued his characteristic gospel invitation to thousands of men and women in a packed stadium. He told those listening to not let another day go by. "Come to Jesus, for in Him, you have everything." People poured out of the stands to give their lives to Christ. The large projection screens showed Billy Graham sitting on a chair behind the podium. And still, more people came forward, hungry to know Jesus. The startling response displayed the real truth about ministry. Ministry is not simply a man or woman doing the work, but Jesus Christ in action. People came forward because the Lord had moved in their hearts. The Lord provided a beautiful message through Billy Graham, and thousands came to know Jesus as a result.

*Lord, work in and through me today to
touch a lost, hurting world. Amen.*

# Christ's Personal Call

Follow Me.

**MATTHEW 4:19**

Seventeen-year-old Amy Carmichael walked down a street of Belfast and noticed a poor, older woman carrying a heavy load. She dropped her own parcels and rushed to help the needy woman. Respectable people in the town stared as she walked down the street with this woman dressed in rags. Amy felt her cheeks grow red with embarrassment. But then the unusual happened in Amy's heart. She heard words from the Bible about work that lasts forever. Feeling convicted, she later locked herself in her room and transacted business with her Lord. She purposed in her heart to follow Jesus regardless of where He led or what He asked. She heard His call and responded, *Yes, Lord, I will follow You.*

When Jesus calls you to follow Him, His invitation is always personal. He custom-designs His approach so He can begin the journey with you, leading you into His plans and purposes. He says, "Follow Me." Will you follow Him today?

*Lord, I will follow You wherever You lead. Amen.*

# Christ's Powerful Call

I will make you fishers of men.

**MATTHEW 4:19**

---

Real ministry never depends on you, but on Christ, who works in and through you. When Jesus said He would make the disciples fishers of men, He was promising them that if they followed Him, He would transform their lives and empower them to become ministers of the gospel.

Jesus will always call you to a work greater than yourself. Your initial response may be, *I can't do that. I'm not enough for the task.* But Jesus never intends for you to do the work. He will *make you* into His servant. He empowers you through the Holy Spirit (Acts 1:8; Ephesians 5:18). He gives you spiritual gifts to use in His service (1 Corinthians 12:4). He transforms you (Romans 12:1-2). He lives in and through you (Galatians 2:20). And finally, He leads and guides you (Romans 8:14). You may respond to His call with fear and trembling, but His work in you will build your confidence in His ability to work through you. You can launch out in ministry knowing your service depends on Him, not on you.

*Lord, thank You for empowering me for ministry.*
*Fill me with courage to follow You today. Amen.*

# Responding to the Call

If anyone wishes to come after Me, he must deny
himself, and take up his cross daily and follow Me.

**LUKE 9:23**

-----------------------------

Your best response to Christ's call might be summed up in one word: *surrender*. When you surrender to Christ, you set aside your own dreams and desires and your rights to personal comfort. Filled anew with Christ's dreams and desires, you launch out on your heart's journey, finding your home in the Lord as you follow Him throughout your lifetime. In the end, you lose nothing and gain everything.

Jesus said, "Whoever loses his life for My sake, he is the one who will save it" (Luke 9:24). You are like a grain of wheat that falls into the earth, dies, and then bears much fruit (John 12:24). Remember when Jesus took five loaves of bread and two fish, blessed the food, and fed 5000 people? Little becomes much in the hands of the Lord. You also will bear much fruit.

*Lord, I surrender to You; use me for Your glory. Amen.*

# A Chance to Die

Whoever wishes to save his life will lose it; but
whoever loses his life for My sake will find it.

**MATTHEW 16:25**

---

Amy Carmichael left the comforts of home in Ireland
and served as a missionary for 53 years in Tamil
Nadu, a state in southeast India. She founded Dohna-
vur Fellowship, a sanctuary for more than 1000 children,
many of whom were rescued from temple prostitution.
She was bedridden the last 20 years of her life because
of an injury. During that time, she wrote many of the
books others have come to know and love.

A young lady aspiring to missionary service once
asked Amy, "What is missionary life like?"

She wrote back, "Missionary life is a chance to die."

There are no shortcuts to following Christ. In God's
economy, no half service will do. When we say, *Yes, Lord,
I will follow You,* we become His missionaries, selflessly
and sacrificially sharing His love with the world.

*Lord, make me Your missionary, Your
ambassador, in every aspect of my life. Amen.*

# The Story of Your Life

Clearly, you are a letter from Christ...This
"letter" is written not with pen and ink, but
with the Spirit of the living God. It is carved not
on tablets of stone, but on human hearts.

**2 CORINTHIANS 3:3 NLT**

Have you ever read a book that was so good, you lost track of time and space and became immersed in its pages? Well, believe it or not, your life is just like that book—a page-turner! God is the author, and He is writing a story on your heart through the Holy Spirit. God's stories are epic, so cultivate a long-term perspective. He writes adventure into your life, so be prepared for surprising twists in the story. He is a meticulous editor, so stay in His Word and respond to the Spirit's work. God is a creative designer, so learn to trust Him. He promotes His writing, so walk through doors He opens in your life. People will read the pages of your life as God's story unfolds in you.

*Lord, keep me faithful as You write
Your story on my heart. Amen.*

# Only One Life

No soldier in active service entangles himself
in the affairs of everyday life, so that he may
please the one who enlisted him as a soldier.

**2 TIMOTHY 2:4**

---

Sir Ernest Shackleton, Antarctic explorer, allegedly placed the following advertisement in a London newspaper in 1912: "Men wanted for hazardous journey, small wages, bitter cold, long months of complete darkness, constant danger, safe return doubtful. Honor and recognition in case of success." Nearly 5000 people (including some women!) responded to his call. They were ready to sacrifice all for the adventure and possible honor.

Jesus calls you into a much higher form of service with a greater sacrifice. You are a soldier of Jesus Christ in active service. Your commitment means you lay aside any entanglements that keep you from serving Him. As has often been said, "Only one life, 'twill soon be past; only what's done for Christ will last." Will you live today with a firm resolve and a steadfast commitment to Christ?

*Lord, show me today how I can engage in
active service for You, free myself of earthly
distractions, and please You. Amen.*

# Finish the Course

But I do not consider my life of any account as dear
to myself, so that I may finish my course and the
ministry which I received from the Lord Jesus.

**ACTS 20:24**

---

Derek Redmond dreamed of winning the 400-meter race in the 1992 Olympic games in Barcelona. When the semi-final qualifying race began, Derek immediately took the lead. But almost halfway into the one-lap race, Derek felt his right hamstring snap. He fell to the ground in pain, and course officials began to make their way toward him. But Derek slowly rose, waved them off, and began limping down the track. When he finally crossed the finish line with the help of his father, the crowd of 65,000 gave him a standing ovation.

You are running a far greater race that includes the ministry you've received from Jesus. You have a great cloud of witnesses cheering you on. Resolve, like Derek and the apostle Paul, to finish your course.

*Lord, help me keep running toward the finish line so*
*I can complete the ministry You have given me. Amen.*

# The Best Words You Will Ever Hear

Well done, good and faithful servant!

**MATTHEW 25:23 NIV**

---

Someday you are going to step from time into eternity and stand face-to-face with your Lord. Your journey with your Lord on earth will be over, but your real life will now begin. Those first moments with Jesus are going to be personal, something intimate between you and Him. Perhaps you will reflect together on many of your shared experiences. Maybe the Lord will think about the good works He prepared beforehand for you to accomplish in His strength. When you are standing in His presence, you will want to know you gave Him your best.

Oswald Chambers called his pursuit of excellence "my utmost for His highest." Today, ask God to help you give your utmost for His highest. More than anything, you will want to hear Jesus say to you, "Well done, good and faithful servant!" Then you will know your faithful service was worth your very best efforts.

*Lord, help me today to give my utmost*
*for Your highest. Amen.*

# A Light Dawned on Earth

The people who were sitting in darkness saw a great light,
And those who were sitting in the land and shadow of death,
Upon them a light dawned.

**MATTHEW 4:16**

---

Darkness always oppresses until it encounters a single ray of light. Then the darkness instantly dissipates.

Do you feel as though you are sitting in darkness today? The prophet Isaiah promised a light would dawn on the people who were in darkness. Matthew confirmed that Jesus is the dawning light for all who are in darkness. When Jesus came to earth, He brought light for those sitting in the oppressive darkness of sin and death. His light leads to eternal life, a quality of existence known to those who enjoy God's rule and reign (John 1:4).

Will you come to the light of Jesus today, receive forgiveness, and inherit eternal life? Will you say no to a life of habitual sin and yes to Christ? Walk in His light every day and experience His blood cleansing you from all your sin (1 John 1:7).

*Lord, may Your light dawn in my darkness, cleanse*
*me from my sin, and give me eternal life. Amen.*

# The Beginning

In the beginning was the Word, and the Word
was with God, and the Word was God.

**JOHN 1:1**

J esus is not only a man; He is also God. John begins his Gospel proclaiming Christ's deity and then gives supporting evidence in subsequent chapters. You cannot read his words accurately and honestly and remain neutral. Either Jesus is who He claimed to be or He was a lunatic or a liar. When you realize Jesus' true identity as God, you are likely to be overwhelmed to know that you can finally see what God is really like. Jesus explains God and is the exact representation of God's nature (John 1:18; Hebrews 1:2-3). John, in awe of Jesus, wrote, "We saw him with our own eyes and touched him with our own hands" (1 John 1:1 NLT).

Today you can know Him too. He is with you even now. Open your heart to Him, meet with Him in the pages of God's Word, and watch your relationship with Him grow.

*Lord, I stand in awe of You today and*
*long to know You more. Amen.*

268

# He Sees You

Before Philip called you, when you
were under the fig tree, I saw you.

**JOHN 1:48**

---

Only God knows the convincing proof each person needs in order to believe in Him. One day Jesus found Philip and said, "Follow Me" (John 1:43). Philip was convinced Jesus was the Messiah that Moses and prophets promised would appear. Philip was so excited, he wanted to tell someone, so he found Nathanael and introduced him to Jesus. Nathanael wondered, "Can any good thing come out of Nazareth?" Philip said, "Come and see." Jesus saw Nathanael from a distance and remarked, "Behold, an Israelite indeed, in whom there is no deceit!" Nathanael was floored. How did Jesus know his heart? Jesus said, "Before Philip called you...I saw you." Nathanael was convinced. Jesus was truly the Messiah.

Will you be a Philip today and invite someone else to "come and see" Jesus? Then, will you be a Nathanael and find great comfort in the fact that Jesus sees you and notices everything about you?

*Lord, thank You for seeing me and knowing me. Amen.*

# New Life

Truly, truly, I say to you, unless one is born
again he cannot see the kingdom of God.

**JOHN 3:3**

Nicodemus was a ruler of the Jews and very religious. Grappling with the finer points of the Mosaic Law was his profession. His life seemed smooth and easy until now. He could not stop thinking about Jesus, a Rabbi who spoke with unusual authority. When Jesus spoke, people listened and responded. Nicodemus noticed and wondered about Jesus. If He was truly sent from God, then He possessed God's authority. He could not be ignored.

Nicodemus was eventually compelled to talk personally with Jesus. He went to Him in the cover of night and asked about His authority. Jesus stepped beyond his question to the heart of His own purpose. "Unless one is born again he cannot see the kingdom of God." New life was the only hope for Nicodemus. And that was why Jesus came to earth—to give new life to Nicodemus and all who believe. Ultimately, Nicodemus believed, and you can too.

*Lord, thank You for giving me new life. Amen.*

# He Will Find You

He had to pass through Samaria.

**JOHN 4:4**

---

One day blended into another for the woman trudging the familiar road to the well. She always drew water at this time to avoid the other women of Sychar, whose disdain for her was painfully obvious. With her history of relational failure, she had lost all hope for respectability.

From afar, she noticed a man sitting at the well. As she approached the well, He immediately engaged her in conversation: "Give Me a drink." But He was not as thirsty as she was. He knew her heart and offered her living water to quench her spiritual thirst and satisfy her with eternal life. Instantly, her mind thought of the Messiah; only He could say such things. Jesus revealed His true identity to her: "I who speak to you am He."

Just think—Jesus *had* to pass through Samaria to give an unlikely woman new life. And you can know that He has to come to where you are to speak with you today.

*Lord, thank You for initiating a life-changing relationship with me. Amen.*

# The Way Is Clear

The veil of the temple was torn in
two from top to bottom.

**MATTHEW 27:51**

---

I n the temple of Jesus' day, the most holy place was
separated from the holy place with a veil. The veil
was so heavy, it required 300 men to set it up. It was as
thick as the palm of a man's hand. When Jesus died on
the cross, the veil in the temple was mysteriously torn
from top to bottom.

What is the significance of that detail—from top
to bottom? How can a 60-foot-tall, 4-inch-thick veil
be torn from the top? Who on earth could possibly
accomplish such a feat 2000 years ago? And why would
anyone tear a veil from the top? The only explanation
is that God Himself tore the veil because He wanted
everyone to know that Jesus cleared the way for man to
experience an intimate relationship with God.

*Lord, thank You for clearing the way that I may know*
*You in an intimate, life-giving relationship. Amen.*

# Jesus Is the Life

I am the way, and the truth, and the life.

**JOHN 14:6**

----------

Open any magazine or watch any television show, and you are bombarded with countless products promising you a better life. If only you have this car, you will be satisfied. Or if you wear a certain makeup, you will find true meaning in life. Jesus sets the record straight about real life: He *is* the life. Life is not found in money, success, possessions, or relationships. Life is found only in Jesus. Cultivate an awareness of Jesus as the true source of life, and you will experience His encouragement and comfort. Remember Him especially when you come into direct contact with opposing views. You may be tempted, especially in difficult times, to try to find satisfaction and meaning in things and people. Many promise life, but only Jesus can deliver on His promise. Learn to run to Jesus in every circumstance, for only in Him will you find true meaning and purpose in life.

*Lord, thank You for being the true life. I am looking to You for meaning, purpose, and true heart satisfaction. Amen.*

# Jesus' Exclusivity

No one comes to the Father but through Me.

**JOHN 14:6**

---

J esus settles forever how you may enjoy a relationship
with God. He claimed to be the only way to God.
His claim is exclusive. Any search for God begins and
ends with Jesus. There is no other name under heaven
by which we must be saved (Acts 4:12). Jesus is the only
answer for your sin and the only way to live forever in
heaven with God.

Anyone who says there is another way to God is saying Jesus' death on the cross was not enough to cover
every sin and open the way to heaven. Come to a firm decision about Jesus' exclusive claim. Once you believe,
you forever settle the main questions of true life. And
you will stand on the firm foundation of the unshake-
able truth of Jesus. Instead of running in many direc-
tions, you will run in only one direction, following
Jesus.

*Lord, thank You for showing me the way*
*to God and to real life. Amen.*

# Burning Hearts

Were not our hearts burning within us while
He was speaking to us on the road, while
He was explaining the Scriptures to us?

**LUKE 24:32**

---

Two discouraged, brokenhearted men walked slowly from Jerusalem toward Emmaus. They had just witnessed Jesus' crucifixion, and their hopes that He was the Messiah died with Him.

While they were walking and talking, a stranger joined them and asked about their conversation. They poured out their hearts, sharing everything they knew about Jesus. The stranger then explained the true meaning of all they had witnessed in Jerusalem. He taught them the truth about the Christ from all the Scriptures, beginning with Moses and the prophets. While He spoke, their hearts burned with passion.

In Emmaus, the stranger took bread, blessed it, and gave it to these two disciples. In that moment, they realized they were with Jesus. With hearts set on fire, they immediately returned to Jerusalem. So too, your heart is set on fire when you meet with Jesus in His Word.

*Lord, today will You set my heart on fire as I*
*open the Word and draw near to You? Amen.*

# Your Road to Emmaus

*Jesus Himself approached and*
*began traveling with them.*

**LUKE 24:15**

-------------------------------

All believers travel the road to Emmaus at some point on their journey. Black clouds of discouragement overcome their hearts. Broken and crushed, their souls are on the road between the cross of Christ and the discovery of new life. Caught in devastating circumstances, they become disillusioned with their lives and wonder what God is doing.

When you experience a time like this, continue living in God's Word, for Jesus will meet you there. He faithfully travels with you on your Emmaus road. He will open the Scriptures and help you understand His Word. He will apply what He says to your hurting heart and will renew and revive you. Jesus sets your heart on fire when you travel with Him on your Emmaus road.

The next time you find yourself on the Emmaus journey, hold your Bible most dear and rely on Jesus to help you.

*Lord, thank You for faithfully meeting me on the*
*Emmaus road and setting my heart on fire. Amen.*

# Take Time with Jesus

They urged Him, saying, "Stay with us..."
So He went in to stay with them.

**LUKE 24:29**

The two men traveling on the road to Emmaus didn't immediately recognize the stranger's true identity. Only when they invited Him to stay awhile were their eyes opened to see Jesus. The lesson for Christ's disciples is clear. Time with Jesus opens your eyes. You will see Jesus as you've never seen Him before. Your spiritual vision will deepen your relationship with the Lord.

Paul prayed for the believers in Ephesus, asking that God would enlighten the eyes of their hearts (Ephesians 1:18). He wanted believers to gain spiritual understanding so they might experience hope, knowledge, and power. The secret to spiritual illumination is time alone with Jesus. The best choice you make every day is to grab your Bible and draw near to the Lord. Time with Jesus will never disappoint. Get ready for awesome views and amazing discoveries.

*Lord, I can't wait to see You as I spend*
*time alone with You. Amen.*

# The Priceless Privilege

I certainly do count everything as loss
compared with the priceless privilege
of knowing Christ Jesus my Lord.

**PHILIPPIANS 3:8 WILLIAMS**

G. Campbell Morgan gave his life to Jesus at the age of ten. He fell in love with Christ and soon dedicated his life to studying God's Word and writing books. His favorite studies focused on Christ. Decades after his conversion, Morgan remarked that he continued to see the Lord Jesus in greater clarity and more amazing glory. He felt totally unworthy to present the majesty and mystery of Christ. Even after 60 years of walking and talking with Christ, Morgan was in awe of His person and His mission.

Jesus is the most awesome, engaging Person you will ever know and love. Paul felt that nothing compared with knowing Christ. He considered knowledge of Christ a priceless privilege. Life is filled with many great pursuits, but knowing Christ is always your most excellent choice.

*Lord, I count all things loss in view of the*
*priceless privilege of knowing You. Amen.*

# Jesus' Generous Heart

What do you want Me to do for you?

**MARK 10:51**

---

Bartimaeus sat by the Jericho road, relegated to a life of begging because he was blind. He heard a crowd approaching and then received the best news in his sad life: Jesus the Nazarene was nearby! "Son of David, have mercy on me!" He cried out again and again, determined to have an audience with the King.

He was not disappointed. Jesus called him over and responded to his cry with shockingly generous words that altered the course of Bartimaeus' life: "What do you want Me to do for you?"

Jesus responded to Bartimaeus on the Jericho road, and He will answer you. And when He answers your cry, He will ask, "What do you want Me to do for you?" Bartimaeus gained his sight the day he met Jesus. You too will receive heaven's greatest gifts from your generous Lord when you cry out to Him.

*Lord, today I am laying out everything I want,*
*assured of Your generous and loving heart. Amen.*

# Abide in Christ

Abide in Me, and I in you.

**JOHN 15:4**

-----

How can you live a fruitful and satisfying life? By staying close to Jesus, your source for everything you need. We are like branches that grow from Jesus, the true Vine. We can grow and bear fruit only when we draw our sustenance from Him. We need to abide in Him, remaining in vital contact with Him. When you stay close to Jesus, receiving all you need from Him, you will experience a rich, meaningful, productive life.

Are you living where God's action is—in the Vine, Jesus Christ? Are you satisfied in Him? Do you see that He is everything you need today? If not, will you run to Him even now? Remember, a branch can do nothing by itself. Without the vine, the branch withers. So remain in vital contact with Jesus and watch your life produce a surprising crop of fruit!

*Lord, today I am running to You for everything I need. Thank You for producing much fruit in my life. Amen.*

# Every Spiritual Blessing in Christ

Blessed be the God and Father of our Lord Jesus
Christ, who has blessed us with every spiritual
blessing in the heavenly places in Christ.

**EPHESIANS 1:3**

A husband and wife saved their money and bought tickets for a cruise. They didn't have any extra money, so they packed their own sandwiches instead of buying meals in the ship's fancy restaurants.

About halfway through the cruise, a steward asked them why they ate sandwiches in their cabin. They explained that they spent all their money on their tickets. When he explained that the meals were included in the ticket price, they headed straight to the nicest restaurant on the ship!

Your union with Christ gives you every spiritual blessing in the heavenly places. Because you are in Christ, you are a spiritual multimillionaire. You have Christ's love, joy, peace, patience, kindness, and so much more. Draw near to Christ today and enjoy all you possess in Him.

*Lord, show me how to enjoy all the spiritual*
*blessings I've received in You. Amen.*

### A Woman's Heart That Dances

Do you long to feel chosen? To partner with the One who can lead you through the intricate steps and turns of your life with a steady, sure hand—and with the assurance of love that will never fail? Join Catherine as she explores the image of the dance, and discover how you can engage in the romance and adventure of an intimate, personal relationship with Christ.

### Six Secrets to a Powerful Quiet Time

If you desire a close walk with God, a rich devotion time, and the joy of pursuing God, you will find inspiration, tools, and encouragement while exploring the *Six Secrets to a Powerful Quiet Time*.